**PRINCE2**™

D1586688

An Introduction to PRINCE2™:
Managing and Directing Successful Projects

London: TSO

Published by TSO (The Stationery Office) and available from:

Online
www.tsoshop.co.uk

Mail, Telephone, Fax & E-mail
TSO
PO Box 29, Norwich, NR3 1GN
Telephone orders/General enquiries: 0870 600 5522
Fax orders: 0870 600 5533
E-mail: customer.services@tso.co.uk
Textphone 0870 240 3701

TSO@Blackwell and other Accredited Agents

Customers can also order publications from:
TSO Ireland
16 Arthur Street, Belfast BT1 4GD
Tel 028 9023 8451 Fax 028 9023 5401

First published 2009

ISBN 9780113311880

Printed in the United Kingdom for The Stationery Office
N6162229 c10 07/09

Contents

List of figures

List of tables

Foreword

The old adage that 'Nothing in this world can be said to be certain, except death and taxes' needs updating to 'Nothing in this world can be said to be certain, except death, taxes and change'! Change has become a way of life as organizations strive to remain competitive and effective. Successful management of business change is therefore a priority in today's highly competitive world. It is against this backdrop that the Office of Government Commerce (OGC) has revised its project management method known as PRINCE2™ (PRojects IN Controlled Environments).

The most noticeable change to PRINCE2 is that there are now two guides: *Managing Successful Projects with PRINCE2* (TSO, 2009) and *Directing Successful Projects with PRINCE2* (TSO, 2009). Together these two publications cover the principles and processes of PRINCE2 but also address the duties and behaviours of those leading project delivery.

This publication, as the title suggests, offers a simple and direct introduction to what PRINCE2 is all about. It is an invaluable guide for both experienced project managers and those new to a PRINCE2 environment. It will be indispensable to those who are just starting in project management, and will serve as an opening to the complexities of project management for the project executive.

An Introduction to PRINCE2 will allow you to understand the basic concepts of project management before tackling the detail contained in the two main guides mentioned above. So whether you are looking for a quick introduction to project management, a short refresher or a handy reference guide, this is the one for you. I can't think of a better place to start.

Jonathan Shebioba

Director

Best Management Practice

Office of Government Commerce

Acknowledgements

The Office of Government Commerce (OGC) acknowledges with thanks the contribution of Sue Taylor (APMG PRINCE2 examiner) in the construction of this guide. In addition, OGC recognizes the contribution of the following individuals who acted as reviewers:

Mike Acaster	Office of Government Commerce
Rachel Buttell	Afiniti Ltd
Anne-Marie Byrne	A-M Byrne Consulting
John Humphries	The Service Station
Lawrie Kirk	Tanner James Management Consultants (Australia)
Nikolaj Raahauge	Peak Consulting Group A/S
Graham Williams	GSW Consultancy Ltd

Particular thanks also go to Jens Wandel, Naoto Yamamoto and John Patterson from the United Nations Development Programme, and Lynne Curran from the Australian Department of Families, Housing, Community Services and Indigenous Affairs, who donated their practical experience to help provide some of the case studies.

OGC would also like to express its gratitude to the Best Practice User Group (BPUG) for their help in coordinating the review.

Introduction

1

1 Introduction

1.1 PURPOSE OF THIS GUIDE

Organizations, whatever their size or market sector, face the continuing challenge of how to transform good ideas into beneficial and tangible outcomes. This guide looks at how projects can help organizations to deliver outcomes which lead to business change, and how effective management of projects is crucial to the delivery of real, measurable benefits. It challenges a common misconception that project management methods are a bureaucratic barrier to achieving change by illustrating how properly applied project management principles can be used to improve the chances of successful delivery.

This guide has been written to introduce the key concepts and elements of the PRINCE2 project management method, which is widely recognized as the industry standard and best practice in project management. PRINCE® stands for 'PRojects IN Controlled Environments'. Based on the original PRINCE method, PRINCE2 was introduced in 1996 in response to user requirements for improved guidance on project management for all projects. It has also been updated in 2009 to ensure it continues to reflect best practice in project management.

This guide provides an overview of the updated PRINCE2 method as documented in the two publications *Managing Successful Projects with PRINCE2* (TSO, 2009) and *Directing Successful Projects with PRINCE2* (TSO, 2009). It introduces the principles, processes and themes, and gives practical examples of applying the method in different situations. It is designed for anyone involved in the management of projects who would like an introduction to and overview of PRINCE2 and how it can be used in practice.

1.2 WHERE DO PROJECTS FIT IN?

Organizations today must be able to balance two different aspects of business: maintaining their current business operations, such as profitability, customer relationships and productivity (business as usual); and changing their business operations in order to survive and compete in the future.

Most organizations have a defined or implied purpose, often articulated in the form of a vision statement, which states the organization's values and goals. These are then broken down into more manageable objectives, each of which will contribute in some way to achieving the overall goals. The objectives will be cascaded throughout the business, measured to assess their success, and their progress regularly reviewed. Projects are not normally undertaken in isolation but will form part of the overall strategy to achieve these organizational objectives and goals.

Depending on the specific environment, projects could be grouped into programmes. These are sets of related projects and activities that together achieve outcomes and realize benefits related to the strategic objectives. Programmes help organizations do the right projects in the right sequence so that the right benefits are achieved in the desired timeframe. Programmes are about realizing the benefits or delivering strategic goals;

projects are about delivering products and services that enable the benefits to be realized.

1.3 WHAT IS A PROJECT?

> A **project** is a temporary organization that is created for the purpose of delivering one or more business products according to an agreed Business Case.

There are a number of characteristics of project work that distinguish it from business as usual:

■ **Change** Projects are the means by which we introduce change

■ **Temporary** As the definition above states, projects are temporary in nature. Once the desired change has been implemented, business as usual resumes (in its new form) and the need for the project is removed. Projects should have a defined start and a defined end

■ **Cross-functional** Projects involve a team of people with different skills working together (on a temporary basis) to introduce a change that will impact others outside the team. Projects often cross the normal functional divisions within an organization and sometimes span entirely different organizations. This frequently causes stresses and strains both within organizations and between, for example, customers and suppliers. Each has a different perspective and motivation for getting involved in the change

■ **Unique** Every project is unique. An organization may undertake many similar projects, and establish a familiar, proven pattern of project activity, but each one will be unique in some way: a different team, a different customer, a different location. All these factors combine to make every project unique

■ **Uncertainty** Clearly, the characteristics already listed will introduce threats and opportunities over and above those we typically encounter in the course of business as usual. Projects are more risky.

A project has a lifecycle, which is the path and sequence through the various activities to produce the final product. The project lifecycle covers the tasks of specifying and designing the product, through to its testing and handover into operational use.

1.4 WHAT IS PROJECT MANAGEMENT?

> Project management is the planning, delegating, monitoring and control of all aspects of the project, and the motivation of those involved, to achieve the project objectives within the expected performance targets for time, cost, quality, scope, benefits and risks.

It is the development of the project's deliverables (known as products in PRINCE2) that deliver the project's results. A new house is completed by creating drawings, foundations, floors, walls, windows, a roof, plumbing, wiring and connected services. None of this is project management – so why do we need project management at all? The purpose of project management is to keep control over the specialist work required to create the project's products or, to continue with the house analogy, to make sure the roofing contractor doesn't arrive before the walls are built.

Additionally, given that projects are the means by which we introduce business change, and that project work entails a higher degree of risk than other business activity, it follows that implementing a secure, consistent, well-proven approach to project management is a valuable business investment.

1.5 WHAT IS PRINCE2?

PRINCE2 is a structured project management method. It is based on experience drawn from thousands of projects, and from the contributions of countless people involved in projects, including project managers, project teams, academics, trainers, consultants and others. It is generic and can be applied to any project regardless of project scale, type, organization, geography or culture.

PRINCE2 covers the management of the project and the management of the resources involved in carrying out the activities of the project. There are six variables involved in any project and, therefore, six aspects of project performance to be managed.

- **Costs** The project has to be affordable and, though we may start out with a particular budget in mind, there will be many factors which can lead to overspending and, perhaps, some opportunities to cut costs
- **Timescales** Allied to this, and probably the next most frequent question asked of a Project Manager, is: 'When will it be finished?'
- **Quality** Finishing on time and within budget is not much consolation if the result of the project doesn't work. In PRINCE2 terms, the project's products must be fit for purpose
- **Scope** Exactly what will the project deliver? Without knowing it, the various parties involved in a project can very often be talking at cross-purposes about this. The customer may assume that, for instance, a fitted kitchen and/or bathroom is included in the price of the house, whereas the supplier views these as extras
- **Risk** All projects entail risks but exactly how much risk are we prepared to accept? Should we build the house near the site of a disused mine, which may be prone to subsidence? If we decide to go ahead, is there something we can do about the risk?
- **Benefits** Perhaps most often overlooked is the question, 'Why are we doing this?' The Project Manager has to have a clear understanding of the purpose of the project as an investment and make sure that what the project delivers is consistent with achieving the desired return.

PRINCE2 is an integrated framework of processes and themes that addresses the planning, delegation, monitoring and control of all these six aspects of project performance.

PRINCE2 does not cover the specialist techniques involved in creating the products, such as design, construction, procurement etc., which will vary widely depending on the type of project. The specialist aspects of any type of project can be easily 'plugged into' the PRINCE2 method and, used alongside PRINCE2, provide a secure overall framework for the project work. PRINCE2 also does not include detailed planning and control techniques such as critical path analysis or earned value analysis; or other aspects of project management such as leadership, motivational and other interpersonal skills.

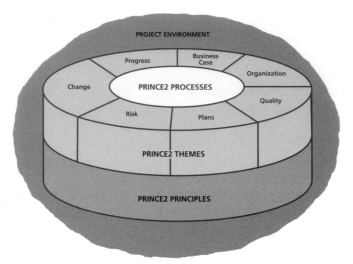

Figure 1.1 The structure of PRINCE2

1.6   PRINCE2 IN CONTEXT

The PRINCE2 method addresses project management from four integrated perspectives, as shown in Figure 1.1.

- **The principles**   These are the guiding obligations and good practices which determine whether the project is genuinely being managed using PRINCE2. There are seven principles, and unless all of them are applied it is not a PRINCE2 project
- **The themes**   These describe aspects of project management that must be addressed continually and in parallel throughout the project. The seven themes explain the specific treatment required by PRINCE2 for various project management disciplines and why they are necessary
- **The processes**   These describe a step-wise progression through the project lifecycle, from getting started to project closure. Each process provides checklists of recommended activities, products and related responsibilities

- **Tailoring PRINCE2 to the project environment**   PRINCE2 is not a 'one size fits all' solution. It is a flexible framework that can readily be tailored to any type or size of project, taking into account factors such as the project size, complexity, geography etc.

1.7   STRUCTURE OF THIS GUIDE

Chapter 2 looks at each of the principles of PRINCE2 and describes why it is important to the method.

Chapter 3 introduces the PRINCE2 themes, and for each one describes:

- Its purpose, benefits and importance
- The major elements which are relevant to the theme.

Chapter 4 summarizes the PRINCE2 journey through a project and the processes used throughout the project lifecycle. The description of each process includes:

- Its purpose and benefits
- The major triggers, key activities and links to other processes
- The main products it produces
- The relevant authorizations and role of the Project Board.

Chapter 5 discusses the main responsibilities of the Project Board throughout a project.

Chapter 6 discusses different types of projects, including projects which form part of a programme, and outlines how PRINCE2 can be tailored appropriately to these different environments.

Throughout the publication, examples are used to illustrate how PRINCE2 can be applied in practice. These show how different sizes and types of organizations can tailor the method to apply it effectively.

1.8 RELATED OGC GUIDANCE

PRINCE2 is part of a suite of guidance developed by the UK Office of Government Commerce (OGC), which is aimed at helping organizations and individuals manage their projects, programmes and services consistently and effectively. Figure 1.2 outlines the structure of the set.

Where appropriate, OGC methods and guidance are augmented by qualification schemes, and all aspects are supported by accredited training and consultancy services. Details of these best-practice guides and other relevant guides can be found in Further Information.

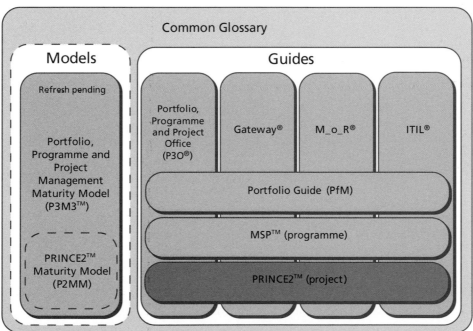

Figure 1.2 OGC best-practice guidance

The PRINCE2 principles

2

2 The PRINCE2 principles

The PRINCE2 principles are the guiding obligations for good project management practice that form the basis of a project being managed using PRINCE2.

The principles provide a framework of good practice for those people involved with a project. They are derived from lessons learned on projects, good and bad, and address many of the most common causes of project failure.

There are seven principles, and unless all of them are applied to a project, it is not being managed using PRINCE2.

- Continued business justification
- Learn from experience
- Defined roles and responsibilities
- Manage by stages
- Manage by exception
- Focus on products
- Tailor to suit the project environment.

2.1 CONTINUED BUSINESS JUSTIFICATION

A PRINCE2 project has continued business justification.

One of the common causes of project failure is a weak business justification. A requirement for a PRINCE2 project is that it has a justifiable reason to start, which is documented and approved and remains valid through its life.

In PRINCE2, the Business Case documents the justification for a project. As a project is inextricably linked to its business justification, the Business Case drives the decision-making processes to ensure that the project remains aligned to the business objectives and benefits being sought.

If, for whatever reason, the project can no longer be justified, the project should be stopped. Stopping a project in these circumstances is a positive contribution to an organization as its funds and resources can be reinvested in other more worthwhile projects.

2.2 LEARN FROM EXPERIENCE

PRINCE2 project teams learn from previous experience: lessons are sought, recorded and acted upon throughout the life of the project.

Projects involve a temporary organization for a finite timescale for a specific business purpose. A common characteristic is that the project includes an element of uniqueness such that it cannot be managed by existing line management or functional units. It is this element of uniqueness that makes projects challenging as the temporary team may not have experience of a project like the one being undertaken.

In PRINCE2, learning from experience permeates the method:

- **When starting a project** Previous or similar projects should be reviewed to see if lessons learned could be applied. If the project is a 'first' for the people within the organization, then it is even more important to learn from others and the project should consider seeking external experience

- **As the project progresses** The project should continue to learn. Lessons should be included in all reports and reviews. The goal is to seek opportunities to implement improvements during the life of the project
- **As the project closes** The project should pass on lessons. Unless lessons provoke change, they are only lessons identified (not learned).

It is the responsibility of everyone involved with the project to **seek** lessons learned rather than waiting for someone else to provide them.

2.3 DEFINED ROLES AND RESPONSIBILITIES

A PRINCE2 project has defined and agreed roles and responsibilities within an organization structure that engages the business, user and supplier stakeholder interests.

Projects involve people. No amount of good planning or control will help if the wrong people are involved, if the right people are not involved, or if people involved do not know what's expected of them or what to expect of others. Lack of an appropriate organization structure is one of the most common causes of project failure.

A project organization is different from a line organization. It may involve resources from different areas of the functional organization, or even different organizations, and have a mix of full-time and part-time resources. To be successful, projects must have an explicit project management team structure, with defined and agreed roles and

responsibilities of people involved in the project and a means for effective communication between them.

Each of the business, user and supplier stakeholder interests (described further in Chapter 3) needs to be represented effectively in the project organization – two out of three is not enough.

2.4 MANAGE BY STAGES

A PRINCE2 project is planned, monitored and controlled on a stage-by-stage basis.

Management stages provide senior management with control points at major intervals throughout the project. At the end of each stage, the project's status should be assessed, the Business Case and plans reviewed to ensure that the project remains viable, and a decision made as to whether to proceed.

Breaking the project into a number of stages enables the extent of senior management control over projects to be varied according to the business priority, risk and complexity involved. Shorter stages offer more control, while longer stages reduce the burden on senior management.

The use of stages also enables planning to be carried out at the correct level. A great deal of effort can be wasted on attempts to plan beyond a sensible planning horizon. For example, a detailed plan to show what each team member is doing for the next 12 months will almost certainly be inaccurate after just a few weeks. A detailed Team Plan for the short term and an outline plan for the long term is a more effective approach: PRINCE2 produces a high-level Project Plan to cover the major products produced throughout the project, and a detailed Stage Plan for the current stage.

2.5 MANAGE BY EXCEPTION

A PRINCE2 project has defined tolerances for each project objective to establish limits of delegated authority.

PRINCE2 enables appropriate governance by defining distinct responsibilities for **directing**, **managing** and **delivering** the project and clearly defining accountability at each level. Accountability is established by:

- Delegating authority from one management level to the next by setting tolerances against six objectives for the respective level of the plan
- Setting up controls so that if those tolerances are forecast to be exceeded, they are immediately referred up to the next management layer for a decision on how to proceed
- Putting an assurance mechanism in place so that each management layer can be confident that such controls are effective.

This is called management by exception, and it reduces the time burden for senior management without removing their control.

2.6 FOCUS ON PRODUCTS

A PRINCE2 project focuses on the definition and delivery of products, in particular their quality requirements.

A successful project focuses on outputs not activities. It agrees and defines the project's products before undertaking the activities required to produce them. The set of agreed products defines the scope of a project and provides the basis for planning and control.

A PRINCE2 project uses Product Descriptions to define details for each product. Product Descriptions provide the means to determine effort estimates, resource requirements, dependencies and activity schedules. Refer to Appendix A for further detail on the content of Product Descriptions.

The 'product focus' supports almost every aspect of PRINCE2: planning, responsibilities, status reporting, quality, change control, scope, configuration management, product acceptance and risk management.

2.7 TAILOR TO SUIT THE PROJECT ENVIRONMENT

PRINCE2 is tailored to suit the project's environment, size, complexity, importance, capability and risk.

The value of PRINCE2 is that it is a universal project management method that can be applied regardless of project type, organization, geography or culture. It can be used by any project because the method is designed to be tailored to its specific needs.

If PRINCE2 is not tailored, it is unlikely that the project management effort and approach are appropriate for the needs of the project. This can lead to 'robotic' project management at one extreme (the method is followed without question) or 'heroic' project management at the other extreme (the method is not followed at all).

Themes 3

3 Themes

The seven PRINCE2 themes (Business Case, Organization, Quality, Plans, Risk, Change, Progress) describe aspects of project management that must be addressed throughout the project's lifecycle, to ensure that the project has:

- A clear **Business Case**
- An appropriate **organization** structure with defined and agreed roles and responsibilities for the project management team
- Built-in **quality** management
- Appropriate **plans**
- A focus on the management of **risk**
- A method to manage potential **change** during the project
- Adequate **progress** controls.

The themes provide guidance on how to perform the different processes through the life of the project.

Examples

Case A

A hurricane affected a country. Thousands of homes were destroyed and people were displaced.

Many international agencies were flown in to help the affected people. One organization took charge of cleaning up the streets that were full of debris and mud. The municipal government was in charge of the emergency response effort, directed the organization where to clean up and clarified what was expected.

The work was inspected to ensure its quality, and the municipal government was informed of the progress. Based on the progress made by the organization and other aid agencies, plans were updated on a daily basis to ensure coordination. At the end of a three-week period, roads were clean and people were able to return to their homes.

Case B

A major flood hit a city. The city was totally destroyed and thousands of people were displaced.

As with case A, many aid agencies joined the emergency response effort. One agency was tasked to build an emergency housing unit, funds were made available and community leaders informed. The government made public land available for the project, but it was 50 km away from the city with no infrastructure or income generation opportunities.

Additional resources were needed to make the new housing units a viable option for the displaced people. Multiple revisions to the project were made, but no decision was taken on the additional funding required. The displaced people complained about the lack of progress and that they had not received what was promised. Six months following the flood there were still no housing units built.

Why are the two examples different?

- Case A had a clear purpose. It was clear what needed to be done, and what the costs would be. Case B had a purpose, but it was not clear how it would be achieved or what effort was required
- Customers' quality expectations were clear in Case A but not in Case B
- The Project Manager role was clear in Case A, whereas Case B suffered from a lack of understanding of who would be managing resources
- Case A identified the risk of uncoordinated aid and took appropriate action, whereas in Case B the risk of not obtaining resources was not managed
- Case A had a clear plan and made adjustments to the plan as it changed while Case B lacked a clear plan
- Case A knew what was done and where the completed work existed, whereas Case B failed to keep track of progress and changes to the project.

These differences had a major impact on whether results were successfully delivered. Case A was successful because:

- It had a clear Business Case
- The outcomes were clearly defined by Product Descriptions and their expected quality, which meant the agencies were able to inspect the work to make sure things were done correctly
- The organization was clearly defined, identifying who was in charge and what was expected
- Responsibilities and ownership were clear
- The work was planned with clear controls through inspection mechanisms

- A risk of overlap of effort was mitigated
- The project kept track of progress by monitoring the products that were completed
- Change was controlled and the plan was adjusted according to progress.

As Case A illustrates, using the PRINCE2 themes can make a significant difference.

3.1 BUSINESS CASE

3.1.1 Why is this important?

> The purpose of the Business Case theme is to establish mechanisms to judge whether the project is (and remains) desirable, viable and achievable as a means to support decision making in its (continued) investment.

It is a PRINCE2 principle that a project must have continued business justification.

The business justification is important as it provides the reasons why the project is being undertaken. Without it no project should start. If business justification is valid at the start of a project, but disappears once it is under way, the project should be stopped or changed.

In PRINCE2, the business justification is documented in a Business Case which describes the reasons for the project based on estimated costs, risks and the expected benefits.

Organizations often have limited resources available to achieve their business objectives. The benefit of the PRINCE2 approach to the Business Case is that it enables organizations to allocate these limited resources to those projects which will provide the greatest business benefits.

Organizations that do not focus on Business Cases proceed with projects even if they have few real benefits or a poor alignment with corporate strategy. Even projects that are compulsory (for example to comply with new legislation) require justification of the option chosen, as there may be several options available that yield different costs, benefits and risks.

3.1.2 What is the PRINCE2 approach?

The Business Case is the key management product from this theme. It is developed at the beginning of the project and maintained throughout the life of the project. It is formally verified by the Project Board at each key decision point, such as the end of each stage, and the continued business justification for the project is confirmed before the project is allowed to proceed. The Business Case is also at the centre of any impact assessment of risks, issues and changes by asking the question, 'How will this affect the viability of the Business Case and the business objectives and benefits being sought?'

Figure 3.1 shows the development path of the Business Case.

The Business Case should contain:

■ The major business **reasons** why the project is needed, and how it will contribute to the achievement of corporate strategies and objectives
■ An analysis of the **business options** available to achieve the objectives
■ A description of the **expected benefits** (positive) or **dis-benefits** (negative) from the project
■ An overview of the project's **timescales**
■ A summary of the overall project **costs**
■ An **investment appraisal** to assess the balance between the development, operations and maintenance costs against the value of the benefits over a period of time
■ A summary of the **major risks** that may affect the project.

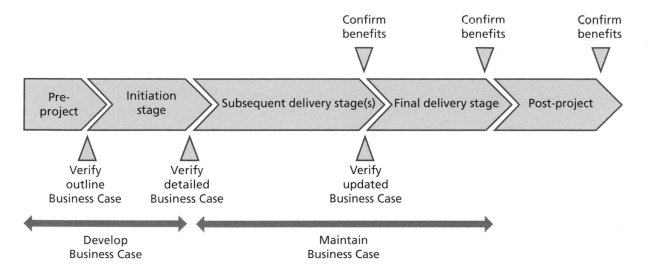

Figure 3.1 The development path of the Business Case

Example

Pharmaceutical companies spend millions of dollars on research and development projects to develop and deliver new drugs onto the market, many of which never actually see the light of day. By maintaining the Business Case and staying focused on the business benefits, these organizations are continually assessing the return on their investment. If, for example, another company delivers a similar drug to market first, significantly reducing the projected market share and financial benefits, the project can be closed and resources redirected to other, more viable projects. Even if significant investment has already been made, why throw good money after bad? If the benefits will not be delivered on one project, it is seen as a strength to be able to focus resources on other projects where they will.

Many forecast benefits that form the basis for a project's approval will not be realized until after the project has closed. To accommodate this, PRINCE2 uses the Business Case to define a Benefits Review Plan, which includes the scope, timing and responsibility for reviews held post-project to measure the benefits realized from the project. The post-project benefits review(s) will also review the performance of the project's products in operational use and identify if there have been any side-effects (good or bad) that may provide useful lessons for other projects.

3.2 ORGANIZATION

3.2.1 Why is this important?

The purpose of the Organization theme is to define and establish the project's structure of accountability and responsibilities.

The Organization theme is important as it ensures that all project personnel understand where they fit and what they are accountable for. The principle of 'defined roles and responsibilities' states that all projects must have defined and agreed roles and responsibilities. Without this, individuals may be unclear as to what they should be doing, delegation of work is difficult and the project may descend into chaos.

A PRINCE2 project will always have three primary categories of stakeholder, and the interests of all three categories must be satisfied if the project is to be successful. Figure 3.2 shows these three interests.

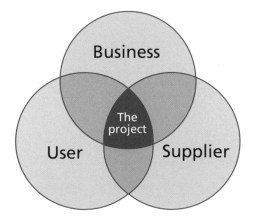

Figure 3.2 The three project interests

The **business** viewpoint ensures that the project meets a business need and provides value for money. The **user** viewpoint represents individuals or groups who will use, support or be impacted by the project's outputs. The **supplier** viewpoint represents those who will produce the project's outputs. The project represents the overlap between the business, user and supplier interests.

If the project management structure does not include representation from all of the three project interests, then problems will appear. For instance, if the business interest is not represented, the project may not fit with the organization's business strategy and may even contradict what the organization and other projects are trying to achieve. If the supplier interest is not represented, the project may not produce the correct products. If the user interest is not represented, the products may not conform to requirements.

3.2.2 What is the PRINCE2 approach?

PRINCE2 defines the project roles and associated responsibilities at the start of the project, and then reviews them at various points during the project to ensure they continue to be effective. Roles can be shared or combined according to the project's needs, but the responsibilities must always be allocated. Figure 3.3 shows the PRINCE2 project management team structure.

- **Corporate or programme management** This sits outside the project management team but is responsible for commissioning the project, providing the project mandate, appointing the Executive and defining the project-level tolerances within which the Project Board must work
- **Project Board** This has authority and responsibility for the project within the

instructions set by corporate or programme management. Chapter 5 contains further details on the duties and behaviours of the Project Board. It consists of three roles:

- *Executive* This role is ultimately accountable for the project's success and is the key decision maker. The Executive is responsible for ensuring that the project is focused on achieving its objectives, delivering a product that will achieve the forecast benefits. The role of the Executive is vested in one individual, so that there is a single point of accountability for the project. Throughout the project, the Executive is responsible for the Business Case
- *Senior User(s)* This role is responsible for specifying the needs of those who will use the project's products and monitoring that the solution will meet those needs. The Senior User commits user resources and monitors products against requirements. The Senior User specifies the benefits and is held to account by demonstrating to corporate or programme management that the forecast benefits that were the basis of project approval are in fact realized. This is likely to involve a commitment beyond the end of the project's life. This role may require more than one person to cover all the user interests, although for the sake of effectiveness it should not be split between too many people
- *Senior Supplier(s)* This role represents the interests of those implementing the project's products, and is responsible for the quality of products delivered by the suppliers and for the technical integrity of the project. The Senior Supplier commits supplier resources. If necessary, more than one person may be required to represent the suppliers

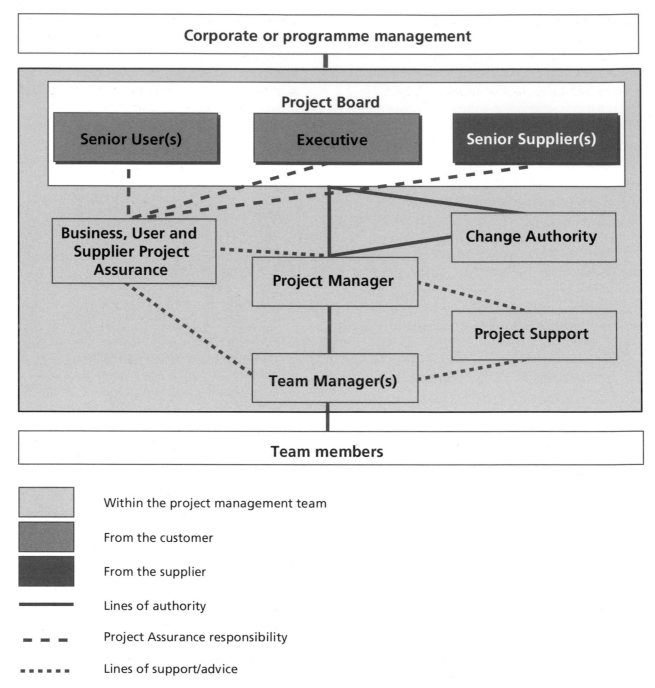

Figure 3.3 Project management team structure

- **Project Assurance** The Project Board is responsible for monitoring all aspects of the project's performance independently of the Project Manager. Project Board members are responsible for Project Assurance aligned to their respective areas of concern – business user or supplier – and may undertake their own Project Assurance tasks or delegate them to different individuals
- **Change Authority** The Project Board is responsible for approving or rejecting requests for change or off-specifications, but may choose to delegate some authority to approve these changes to a separate Change Authority
- **Project Manager** The Project Manager is the single focus for day-to-day management of the project and has the authority, within specified constraints, to run the project on behalf of the Project Board. The Project Manager manages the Team Managers and Project Support, and is responsible for liaison with Project Assurance and the Project Board. In projects with no separate individual allocated to a Team Manager role, the Project Manager will be responsible for managing work directly with the team members involved. In projects with no separate Project Support role, the support tasks also fall to the Project Manager, although they may be shared with team members. In a PRINCE2 environment the Project Manager role should not be shared
- **Team Manager** The Team Manager's prime responsibility is to ensure production of those products allocated by the Project Manager. The Team Manager reports to, and takes direction from, the Project Manager
- **Project Support** The Project Manager is responsible for carrying out Project Support, but some of this work can be delegated to a separate Project Support role. This may include providing administrative services, or advice and guidance on the use of project management tools. Project Support is also responsible for administering any configuration management procedure and tools for the project.

> **Example**
>
> The project to produce the PRINCE2:2009 manual (*Managing Successful Projects with PRINCE2*, TSO, 2009) was run using PRINCE2. The Executive was represented by OGC as the sponsoring organization. The Senior User was represented by the Best Practice User Group. There were two Senior Suppliers, one from APM Group (for the supporting qualifications) and one from The Stationery Office (TSO), the manual's publisher. Three Team Managers reported to the Project Manager: a lead author for the authoring team, a TSO representative for the publication production team and an APM Group representative for the qualification development teams.

A successful project organization also needs an effective strategy to manage communication flows to and from key stakeholders internal and external to the project. The Organization theme covers this by developing a Communication Management Strategy for the project. This contains a description of the means and frequency of communication to parties both internal and external to the project.

During a project, corporate or programme management retains control by receiving project information as defined in the Communication Management Strategy and taking decisions on project-level exceptions escalated by the Project Board.

3.3 QUALITY

3.3.1 Why is this important?

> The purpose of the Quality theme is to define and implement the means by which the project will create and verify products that are fit for purpose.

The Quality theme is important to ensure that the project creates and verifies products which are fit for purpose. Effort invested in a project will be wasted if the project fails to deliver what the business and users need. Once under way, a project will come under pressure on timescales, resources and funding, and it is all too easy to take short-cuts with the quality of the outputs.

The 'focus on products' principle is central to PRINCE2's approach to quality. It provides a common understanding of what the project will create (the scope) and the criteria against which the project's products will be assessed (the quality). Without this, the project would be exposed to major risks (such as acceptance disputes, rework or uncontrolled change), which could weaken or invalidate the Business Case.

Defining quality criteria for products enables the quality management activities to be determined and the true cost and timescale for the project to be understood. Underestimating or omitting quality management activities is likely to lead to slippages, overspends and/or poor quality results.

3.3.2 What is the PRINCE2 approach?

PRINCE2 applies two major elements to quality throughout a project.

3.3.2.1 Quality planning

This involves:

- Understanding the customer's quality expectations. These cover the key quality requirements for the project product, any standards and processes to be applied, and any measurements that may be useful to assess whether the project product meets the quality requirements
- Defining the project's acceptance criteria. This is a prioritized list of measurable definitions of the attributes required for the products to be acceptable to key stakeholders
- Documenting the customer's quality expectations and acceptance criteria in the Project Product Description (described further in Appendix A)
- Formulating a Quality Management Strategy, which describes how the quality management systems will be applied to the project and outlines the standards, techniques, procedures and tools to be used
- Creating Product Descriptions for the project's products, which include quality criteria, quality methods and quality responsibilities, for the major project products
- Creating a Quality Register to hold details of all quality events planned and undertaken during the project.

3.3.2.2 Quality control

This involves implementing and tracking the quality methods defined. It is achieved by implementing, monitoring and recording the quality methods and responsibilities defined in the Quality Management Strategy and Product Descriptions. It includes:

■ Carrying out the quality methods using quality inspections or testing techniques such as the PRINCE2 quality review technique
■ Maintaining the quality and approval records, including updating the Quality Register with quality activities
■ Gaining acceptance.

Example

Everyone involved in the creation of a product must have a common understanding of its purpose and the standards to which it must adhere in order to be 'fit for purpose'. Consider, for example, a project to build a new mobile phone for global use. Suppose that the range of temperatures the phone must operate within is not specified as part of its quality criteria. The phone might work very well in extreme cold, but may fail quickly in high-temperature environments. Without articulating quality criteria to measure against, this aspect of 'fit for purpose' in high-temperature environments would never be achieved.

Figure 3.4 outlines the path to quality through the project.

Many organizations provide assurance independent of the project, to ensure that the quality methods being applied to the project conform to corporate or programme management standards. This is called quality assurance and is outside the scope of PRINCE2. Quality assurance is different from Project Assurance, which is conducted within the project and is a responsibility of the Project Board to ensure that the project is conducted properly.

Example

A large Australian government department was responsible for protecting and supporting a high-profile building, renowned for its architecture and emphasis on quality fittings. In this environment it was important to ensure that quality standards for the overall building were not compromised. All proposals involving infrastructure change needed not only to comply with departmental quality requirements but also to ensure that the design integrity of the building was maintained.

In order to ensure that small (and seemingly irrelevant) changes to the quality of the internal infrastructure did not create a cumulative decline in the overall integrity of the building design, each project's Quality Management Strategy incorporated the relevant departmental quality requirements. As the Quality Management Strategy was developed before a project was planned in detail, the approach to quality could be built into the plans for the project and implemented effectively in order to maintain the overall quality of the building.

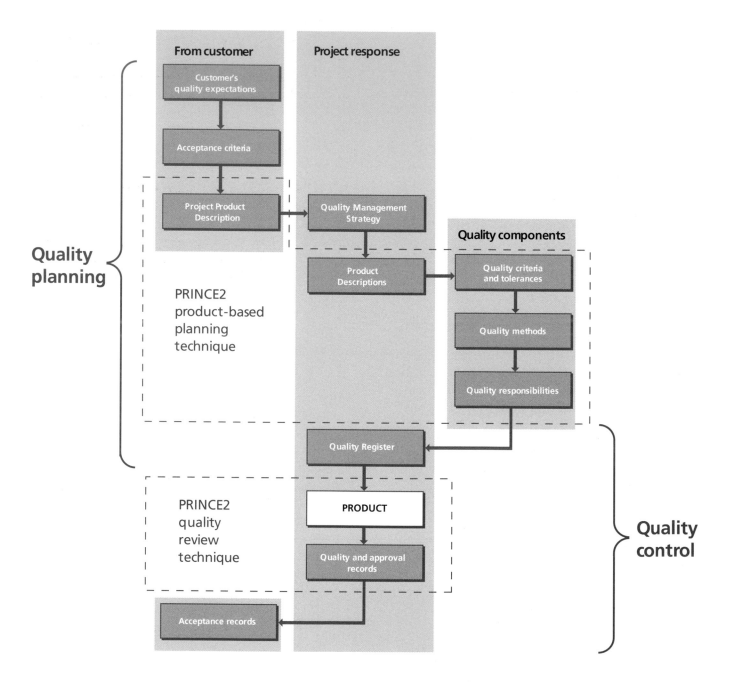

Figure 3.4 The quality audit trail

3.4 PLANS

3.4.1 Why is this important?

> The purpose of the Plans theme is to facilitate communication and control by defining the means of delivering the products (the where and how, by whom, and estimating the when and how much).

The Plans theme is important as it defines the details for how the project's products will be delivered. Managers need confidence to commit resources to a project when the benefits may be a long way off. Planning replaces the hope that something will be delivered with a map showing how it can be accomplished.

Effective project management relies on effective planning, as without a plan there can be no control. Planning provides everyone involved in the project with information on what is required and how, when and by whom it will be achieved. It helps to identify whether the targets are achievable. The very act of planning helps the project management team to 'mentally rehearse the project', enabling omissions, duplication, threats and opportunities to be identified and managed.

Plans also provide a baseline against which progress can be measured. They enable planning information to be communicated in order to secure any commitments which underpin the plan.

Planning is vital to the success of any project. It is often overlooked due to pressure to achieve results and to get work done. However, it is counterproductive to produce products that are later found to be unnecessary, out of order or unfit for purpose.

3.4.2 What is the PRINCE2 approach?

The 'product focus' principle underpins the PRINCE2 approach to planning. This means that the products required are identified first, followed by the activities, dependencies and resources required to deliver those products. PRINCE2 uses the technique of product-based planning to produce all the levels of plan required in a project.

It is not usually either desirable or possible to plan an entire project in detail at the start: plans need to be produced at different levels of scope and detail. PRINCE2 recommends three levels of plan, the Project Plan, the Stage Plan and the Team Plan (shown in Figure 3.5), to reflect the needs of the different levels of management involved in the project.

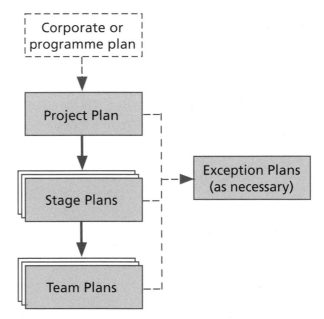

Figure 3.5 PRINCE2's planning levels

- **Project Plan** This is created at the start of the project and provides an overall view of how and when a project's time, cost, scope and quality performance targets are to be achieved, by showing the major products, activities and resources required throughout the project
- **Stage Plans** These are created during the project for each management stage, and should provide sufficient detail for the Project Manager to use as the basis for day-to-day control of a management stage
- **Team Plans** These are optional, but if used will be produced by a Team Manager when executing one or more Work Packages
- **Exception Plans** These are prepared to show the actions required to recover from the effect of a tolerance deviation.

Figure 3.6 shows the steps required to produce a PRINCE2 plan. These steps can be summarized as follows:

- **Design the plan** Decide how the plan can best be presented given its audience and how it will be used
- **Define and analyse the products** Identify, define and analyse the project's products, using the PRINCE2 technique of product-based planning. This technique includes the following steps:
  - Write the Project Product Description, which defines the scope of the project and what it must deliver to obtain customer acceptance
  - Create the product breakdown structure, breaking down the Project Product Description into its constituent sub-products
  - Write the Product Descriptions, describing each of the sub-products and their quality criteria

Example

A Project Plan can have significant value as a communication tool to inform teams and team members of what has been done and what needs to be done, by whom and when.

Many organizations use a project definition workshop to kick-start the planning process. In one example, 20 key stakeholders were invited to attend a facilitated workshop to develop a plan for a project to deliver an organization's new IT strategy. The facilitator outlined the 'vision' for the product – a document that would provide the basis for delivering the IT strategy – then asked the question, 'How do we get here?' The aim of the question was to gather a list of products that would form the basis of a high-level plan to deliver the product. Each product volunteered by the stakeholders was written on a note and placed at an appropriate point on a timeline sketched across a series of tables. At the end of this workshop, high-level products like the chapter heading for the strategy were captured, along with other supporting products.

  - Create the product flow diagram, defining the sequence of development of the products in the plan and any dependencies between them
- **Identify activities and dependencies** Identify the activities required to create each of the planned products, and any dependencies between activities and products
- **Prepare estimates** Identify the resource types required and estimate the effort required for each activity

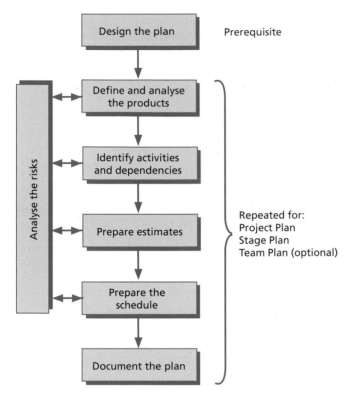

Figure 3.6 The PRINCE2 approach to plans

- **Prepare the schedule** Define the sequence of activities, assign actual resources, define milestones and control points and present the schedule
- **Analyse the risks** Review products, resources and activities to identify potential risks
- **Document the plan** Consolidate the plan information and present it to the appropriate audience.

Example

The Department of Families, Housing, Community Services and Indigenous Affairs, an Australian federal government department, successfully used product-based planning on a 12-month project involving the national roll-out of a new information system. Over 20 business, user and supplier representatives attended a detailed planning day, at which attendees were able to clarify quality requirements and produce a product breakdown structure and product flow diagram. The process was assisted by the active involvement and guidance of both the project Executive and the Senior Supplier at a crucial time during the workshop.

The product flow diagram created by this process was robust enough to remain unchanged throughout the project. It proved to be an extremely effective tool for communicating what the project was to produce, showing the interdependencies of products and highlighting the crucial decision points (stage boundaries). Product Descriptions were also invaluable when communicating the requirements of the Project Board and documenting what the project had to create, and showed that quality criteria were real and would be checked in all of the project's products.

3.5   RISK

3.5.1 Why is this important?

> The purpose of the Risk theme is to identify, assess and control uncertainty and, as a result, improve the ability of the project to succeed.

The Risk theme is important as it seeks to manage uncertain events which, if they occur, will throw the project off its planned course. Being prepared for these events, by identifying their possible impacts and planning how best to respond to them, gives the project a better chance of achieving a successful outcome.

A risk is an uncertain event that could have an impact on the achievement of objectives, either negative (a threat) or positive (an opportunity). Risk taking in projects is inevitable since projects are enablers of change, and change introduces uncertainty. The PRINCE2 approach to managing risks improves the ability of the project to succeed, by identifying, assessing and controlling risks.

Management of risk is a continual activity, performed throughout the life of the project. Without an ongoing and effective risk management procedure it is not possible to be confident that the project is able to meet its objectives and therefore whether it is worthwhile for it to continue. Effective risk management therefore is a prerequisite of the 'continued business justification' principle.

3.5.2 What is the PRINCE2 approach?

A risk consists of a combination of the probability of a threat or opportunity occurring and the magnitude of its impact on objectives.

The PRINCE2 approach to managing risks on a project consists of five steps, shown in Figure 3.7.

- **Identifying** the procedures, responsibilities and reporting requirements for the project (documented in the Risk Management Strategy), and the individual threats or opportunities which may face the project (documented in the Risk Register)
- **Assessing** the probability, impact and proximity of the threats and opportunities, both for individual risks and in total to show the net effect of all the identified threats and opportunities facing the project
- **Planning** appropriate responses to the risks identified in order to remove or reduce the threats and maximize the opportunities
- **Implementing** the planned responses, monitoring their effectiveness and taking corrective action where necessary
- **Communicating** information related to the risks to interested parties.

The first four steps are sequential with the 'communicate' step running in parallel, as the findings of any of the other steps may be communicated prior to the completion of the overall process. All of the steps are iterative – when additional information becomes available, it is often necessary to revisit earlier steps and carry them out again.

Example

Imagine sending an entire project team from Europe to North America to attend a seminar, all scheduled to fly together. There is a risk that bad weather may cause the aeroplane to crash, resulting in the entire workforce being lost. Assessing this risk, the probability may be low but the impact on the project in terms of time, cost, quality, benefits and resources would be very high. There are a number of possible responses: avoid the risk by not letting them go; reduce the risk by not letting them all go or sending them on separate flights; create a fallback plan to recruit and train new staff if the risk occurs; transfer some of the financial impact by taking out insurance; or accept the risk and hope for the best. In this case, based on the cost of the action versus the probability and impact of the risk actually occurring, the most suitable response would probably be to accept or reduce the risk. This would then need to be planned and implemented, perhaps by changing the travel bookings to separate the travellers, and the strategies communicated to all the people involved.

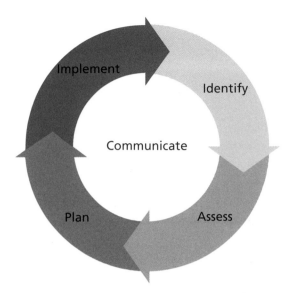

Figure 3.7 The risk management procedure

products which will inevitably arise through the life of a project. Every project needs a method of identifying, assessing and controlling issues that may result in change. Without an effective change control procedure, a project may quickly drift out of control. The aim of change control is not to prevent changes, but to ensure that every change is agreed by the relevant authority before it takes place.

3.6 CHANGE

3.6.1 Why is this important?

The purpose of the Change theme is to identify, assess and control any potential and approved changes to the baseline.

The Change theme is important as it defines a controlled method of dealing with the changes to

3.6.2 What is the PRINCE2 approach?

The PRINCE2 approach to change consists of configuration management and issue/change control.

3.6.2.1 Configuration management

Effective control of changes is only possible if it is underpinned by a configuration management system which ensures that products are baselined and controlled, and that the correct versions are delivered. Configuration management typically comprises the following core activities:

- **Planning** Deciding the level of configuration management required for the project, planning how it will be achieved and documenting this in the Configuration Management Strategy
- **Identification** Specifying and identifying all components of the project's products and establishing a coding system to uniquely identify products
- **Control** Approving and baselining products, then ensuring that changes are made only with the agreement of the appropriate authorities
- **Status accounting** Reporting current and historical data concerning each product
- **Verification and audit** Comparing the actual status of products against the authorized state, looking for any discrepancies, and checking that the configuration management procedure is being undertaken in accordance with the Configuration Management Strategy.

3.6.2.2 Issue and change control

PRINCE2 provides an approach to dealing with any issues that come to light during a project. Figure 3.8 outlines this approach.

- **Capture** Undertake an initial analysis to determine the type of issue that has been raised and whether it can be managed informally or formally. Issues being managed formally should be entered in the Issue Register and given a unique identifier. An Issue Report should be created to capture what is already known about the issue. Issues being handled informally can be tracked through the Daily Log
- **Examine** Undertake an impact analysis to consider the impact the issue may have on the project performance targets, Business Case, and risk profile

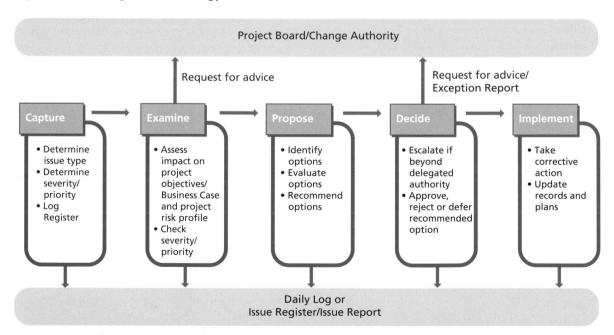

Project Board/Change Authority

Request for advice

Request for advice/
Exception Report

Capture	Examine	Propose	Decide	Implement
• Determine issue type • Determine severity/ priority • Log Register	• Assess impact on project objectives/ Business Case and project risk profile • Check severity/ priority	• Identify options • Evaluate options • Recommend options	• Escalate if beyond delegated authority • Approve, reject or defer recommended option	• Take corrective action • Update records and plans

Daily Log or
Issue Register/Issue Report

Figure 3.8 Issue and change control procedure

- **Propose**   Consider alternative options for responding to an issue and propose a course of action to take
- **Decide**   Resolve the issue or escalate to the Project Board or its delegated Change Authority for a decision
- **Implement**   Take the necessary corrective action, such as updating or issuing a Work Package, or creating an Exception Plan for approval by the Project Board.

PRINCE2 uses the term 'issue' to cover any concern, query, request for change, suggestion or off-specification raised during a project. Table 3.1 describes these further.

Example

A good example of controlling change is to see the impact of it during a house renovation.

At the start of the project, the architect sends the customer detailed draft plans showing where all the electrical sockets are to be positioned. The customer indicates on the plans that they would like three sockets to be moved to a new location. They then send the plans back to the architect for modification so that they can be sent out to prospective builders to obtain quotations.

Does this require change control? Although the drawing needs to be changed to reflect the new positioning of the sockets, it is not change control because it is part of the drafting process. What is required is effective configuration management.

After the builder has been engaged, but before the work has started, the customer decides that they would like to have the sockets and switches made from brass – not plastic, as per the existing specification.

Does this require change control? Although the work has not started, the specification has been changed and the builder will have quoted a price based on the original specification. Therefore it is essential that the builder agrees to the request for change, which is dependent on the customer agreeing to pay the additional amount.

After the builder has completed the electrical work, the customer notices that two of the sockets are not in the right location.

Does this require change control? Although the work is complete, it does not meet the agreed specification. This is known as an off-specification. As the customer clearly specified requirements and the builder agreed to them, corrective action is required by the builder at their own cost.

3.7   PROGRESS

3.7.1 Why is this important?

The purpose of the Progress theme is to establish mechanisms to monitor and compare actual achievements against those planned; provide a forecast for the project objectives and the project's continued viability; and control any unacceptable deviations.

The Progress theme is important as it monitors and compares actual achievements against those planned. A plan showing how to get from the start to the end of a project is only part of the picture.

Table 3.1 Types of issue

Types of issue	Definition	Examples
Request for change	A proposal for a change to a baseline.	The Senior User would like to increase the capacity of a product from 100 to 150 users.
Off-specification	Something that should be provided by the project, but currently is not (or is forecast not to be) provided. This might be a missing product or a product not meeting its specification.	Advice from a supplier that they can no longer deliver one of the products specified by the customer.
Problem/concern	Any other issue that the Project Manager needs to resolve or escalate.	Advice from a Team Manager that a team member has been taken ill and as a result the target end date for a Work Package will slip by a week.
		Notification that one of the suppliers has gone bankrupt, resulting in the need to identify and engage a new supplier.

There also needs to be a means of identifying progress through the plan and what to do if the project is deviating from its path.

The 'manage by exception' principle states that a project should have clear responsibilities for directing, managing and delivering the project, setting tolerances for project objectives to establish limits of delegated authority. Control of progress is all about decision making and is central to project management, ensuring that the project remains viable against its approved Business Case.

3.7.2 What is the PRINCE2 approach?

Progress control involves measuring the actual progress against the performance targets of time, cost, quality, scope, benefits and risk, and then using this information to make decisions (such as whether to approve a stage or Work Package, whether to escalate deviations, whether to prematurely close the project etc.) and to take actions as required. PRINCE2 provides progress control through:

- **Delegating authority** from one level of management to the level below. Tolerances define the amount of discretion that each management level can exercise without the need to refer up to the next level for approval, and by default authorize actions to occur if they remain within tolerance. Progress is measured against the allowable tolerances, and escalated to the next level of management if any tolerance is forecast to be exceeded. Allocation of tolerances follows the four levels of project organization as shown in Figure 3.9

- **Dividing the project into management stages** and authorizing the project one stage at a time. Management stages are partitions of the project with management decision points. A management stage is a collection of activities and products whose delivery is managed as

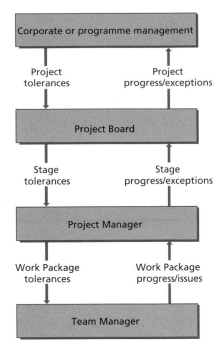

Figure 3.9 Delegating tolerance and reporting actual and forecast progress

a unit, and is the element of work that the Project Manager is managing on behalf of the Project Board at any one time. The number and size of management stages depends on the scale and risk of the project – stages should be shorter when there is greater risk, uncertainty or complexity, and longer when risk is lower

■ **Event-driven and time-driven progress reporting** and reviews. Event-driven controls take place when a specific event, such as the end of a stage, occurs. Time-driven controls take place at pre-defined intervals, for example producing monthly Highlight Reports

■ **Raising exceptions** to the next higher level of management when the Work Package, stage or project is forecast to exceed its tolerances.

The Project Board delegates the authority for day-to-day control of a stage, within agreed tolerances, to the Project Manager. As long as the stage is forecast to remain within tolerance the Project Manager has discretion to make adjustments as required. This allows the Project Board to manage by exception, retaining the level of control it requires while reducing the administrative overhead of being involved.

Example

Assume the same project to construct 20 schools is being undertaken in two different provinces (A and B) in a country. Each project is scheduled to take three years, but the two projects have their own plans, approaches and management arrangements based on the specific needs of each province.

The project in province A will have three stages over three years, with the first one-year stage planned to deliver the first five schools. Tolerance is set at +50% / –10% cost and +50% / –2% schedule for the first stage, with monthly Highlight Reports. The project in province B has a first stage of six months to deliver three schools, with +1% / –1% cost and +5% / –5% schedule tolerance, with weekly Highlight Reports.

What are the reasons and implications of these differences? The project in province A has a 'looser' set of controls, which may be justified based on the level of experience of the Project Manager, the work team, the environment etc.

Likewise, the 'tighter' controls in province B might be a result of a less experienced Project Manager or team, or higher risks associated with the project. All things being equal in both provinces, the project in province B will have more opportunities to control and guide the project.

The way PRINCE2 handles exceptions depends on the implementation of tolerances, i.e. the permissible deviation above and below a plan's target without escalating the deviation to the next level of management. These can be set for each of the six performance targets of time, cost, quality, scope, benefit and risk, and applied at project, stage and team levels.

Processes

4

4 Processes

PRINCE2 is a process-based approach for project management. A process is a structured set of activities designed to accomplish a specific objective, and takes one or more defined inputs and turns them into defined outputs. There are seven processes in PRINCE2, which provide the set of activities required to successfully direct, manage and deliver a project. Each process produces a number of key management products.

Figure 4.1 shows the PRINCE2 processes and how they are used during the life of a project. Figures 4.2 to 4.6 show how the processes interface with each other, with the main process for each section

(e.g. Starting up a Project in Figure 4.2) appearing in **bold type**. All other conventions regarding the shape and shading of the diagram components are as per the main PRINCE2 manual.

4.1 THE PRINCE2 JOURNEY

4.1.1 Pre-project

In the beginning, someone has an idea or a need. This could arise from almost anything, such as the need to respond to competitive pressures or changes to legal conformance requirements. In PRINCE2, the trigger for a project is called

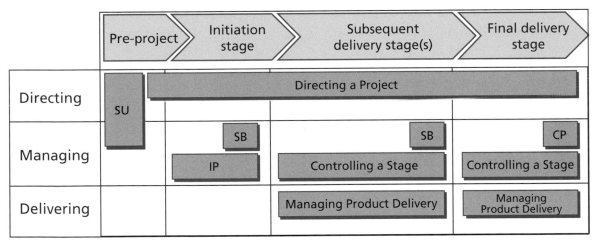

Key
SU = Starting up a Project
IP = Initiating a Project
SB = Managing a Stage Boundary
CP = Closing a Project

Note
- Starting up a Project is used by both the directing and managing levels.
- There should be at least two management stages, the first of which is the initiation stage.
- Managing a Stage Boundary is first used at the end of the initiation stage and repeated at the end of each subsequent stage except the final stage. It is also used to prepare Exception Plans, which can be done at any time including in the final stage.
- For complex or lengthy initiations, Controlling a Stage and Managing Product Delivery can optionally be used to manage the initiation stage.

Figure 4.1 The PRINCE2 processes

a project mandate. This is provided by the sponsoring organization (corporate or programme management) and can vary in detail – from a verbal instruction to a detailed project definition.

Before the detailed work to scope the project is carried out, it is important to verify that the project is viable and that it is worth continuing with initiation. PRINCE2 covers this during the process Starting up a Project, which, by producing a Project Brief which outlines the major scope, costs and benefits of the project, gives the Project Board sufficient detail to make its first control decision, either to continue work on the project or to stop before expending more resources and effort.

4.1.2 Initiation stage

Once there is a decision to go ahead, the project needs to be planned in detail. Funding has to be obtained and controls should be defined to ensure that the project proceeds in accordance with the wishes of those people paying for the project and those who will make use of what the project delivers. The detailed planning, establishment of the project management strategies and controls, development of a robust Business Case and a means of reviewing benefits are covered by the Initiating a Project process.

The initiation stage culminates in the production of the Project Initiation Documentation which is reviewed by the Project Board to decide whether to authorize the project. As the contents of the Project Initiation Documentation are likely to change throughout the project (under change control), this version of the Project Initiation Documentation is preserved as input for later performance reviews.

4.1.3 Subsequent delivery stages

The Project Board delegates day-to-day control of the project to the Project Manager on a stage-by-stage basis. The Project Manager needs to assign work to be done, ensure that the outputs of such work (products) meet relevant specifications and gain approval where appropriate. The Project Manager also needs to ensure that progress is in line with the approved plan and that the forecast for the performance targets are within agreed tolerances. The Project Manager ensures that a set of project records are maintained to assist with progress control, and informs the Project Board of progress through regular reports. The activities to control each stage are covered by the Controlling a Stage process.

In the Managing Product Delivery process, the Team Manager(s) or team members execute assigned Work Packages (which will deliver one or more products) and keep the Project Manager appraised of progress.

Towards the end of each management stage the Project Manager requests permission to proceed to the next stage by reporting how the stage performed, providing an update to the Business Case and planning the next management stage in detail. The Project Manager provides the information needed by the Project Board in order for it to assess the continuing viability of the project and to make a decision to authorize the next management stage. The activities to manage each stage boundary are covered in the Managing a Stage Boundary process.

4.1.4 Final delivery stage

As a project is a temporary undertaking, during the final stage (once the Project Manager has gained approval for all the project's products) it is time to decommission the project. The Project Board needs to be satisfied that the recipients of the project's products are in a position to own and use them on an ongoing basis. Should this be the case, the products can be transitioned into operational use and the project can close. The project documentation should be tidied up and archived, the project should be assessed for performance against its original plan and the resources assigned to the project need to be released. The closure activities include planning post-project benefits reviews to take place for those benefits that can only be assessed after the products have been in use (and therefore after the project has closed). The activities to decommission a project are covered by the Closing a Project process.

4.1.5 Directing a Project

The Project Board sets direction and makes decisions throughout the life of the project. The purpose of the Directing a Project process is to enable the Project Board to exercise overall control of the project while delegating its day-to-day management to the Project Manager – in other words to manage by exception. It starts on completion of the Starting up a Project process and is triggered by the request to initiate a project. The

Project Board authorizations in Directing a Project are included in the descriptions of the relevant processes.

4.2 STARTING UP A PROJECT

4.2.1 Why is this important?

The purpose of the Starting up a Project process is to answer the question 'Do we have a viable and worthwhile project?' before conducting the work to scope and plan the project at a detailed level. The Starting up a Project process should be conducted at a high level: its aim is to do the minimum necessary to decide whether it is worthwhile to initiate a project.

4.2.2 Where does it fit and what happens?

In PRINCE2 terms, the trigger for the start-up of a project is called the project mandate. This comes from corporate or programme management and could be at almost any level of detail – if the project is part of a programme it is likely that most information will come from the programme and little more will be required, but sometimes the mandate can be as brief as a telephone call, so

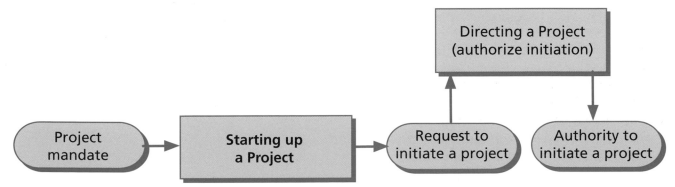

Figure 4.2 Where does Starting up a Project fit?

more detailed analysis will be needed. The purpose of the Starting up a Project process is to provide the Project Board with enough information to enable it to make the decision whether to proceed with the detailed scoping of the project.

It comprises the following activities:

- Appoint the Executive and the Project Manager
- Capture previous lessons
- Design and appoint the project management team
- Prepare the outline Business Case
- Select the project approach and assemble the Project Brief
- Plan the initiation stage.

4.2.3 What is produced?

Management products produced during this process include:

- **Project Brief** This is the main output from this process. The Project Brief includes a definition of the project scope and desired outcomes, the initial version of the Project Product Description (a special form of Product Description containing the customer's quality expectations and the acceptance criteria and acceptance methods for the overall project), outline Business Case, project approach (which defines the solution or method to be used to create the Project Product) and details of the project organization. It is the document that the Project Board will use to approve project initiation. During the Initiating a Project process it will be refined further to produce the Project Initiation Documentation. See Appendix A for suggested contents for the Project Brief
- **Project management team** The Project Board, Project Manager and other members of the project management team should be appointed during this process
- **Lessons Log** Any lessons that can be learned from previous projects should be documented in the Lessons Log
- **Daily Log** This is created to hold details of any project information which is not yet being captured elsewhere
- **Stage Plan** The detailed Stage Plan showing the timescales and resources needed for the initiation stage will form part of the approval from the Project Board.

The Project Board reviews the Project Brief, decides whether to initiate the project and states the levels of authority to be delegated to the Project Manager for the initiation stage.

Example

In the UN Development Programme's start-up process, the Project Brief is developed after a series of consultations with the stakeholders. It is appraised by the Project Appraisal Committee to make sure the project adequately addresses the needs. The Project Appraisal Committee also appoints the project executive group, which will serve as the Project Board during the rest of the project. In this way, the organization balances participation and executive decision making. Once the executive group is formed, it approves the next Stage Plan.

Table 4.1 outlines the roles which are responsible for completing the activities relevant to this process.

Table 4.1 Starting up a Project: roles

Role	Responsibility
Corporate or programme management	Appointing the Executive
Executive	Appointing the Project Manager
	Capturing previous lessons
	Designing and appointing the project management team
	Preparing the outline Business Case
Project Manager	Capturing previous lessons
	Designing and appointing the project management team
	Reviewing the outline Business Case
	Selecting the project approach and assembling the Project Brief
	Planning the initiation stage

4.2.4 Directing a Project – authorize initiation

The purpose of authorizing initiation is to check the viability of the project before committing funds and resources to initiate it. Towards the end of the Starting up a Project process, the Project Manager will request authorization for the funds and resources required to initiate the project. The Project Board members consider the authorization based on two documents, the Project Brief and the Initiation Stage Plan.

To authorize initiation, the Project Board will collectively undertake the following responsibilities.

Actions required for authorizing initiation

Review and approve the Project Brief:

- Confirm the project definition and approach
- Review and approve the Project Product Description
- Formally confirm the appointments to the core project management team
- Review and approve the outline Business Case, particularly the projected business benefits.

Approve the Initiation Stage Plan:

- Approve the plan to develop the Project Initiation Documentation
- Obtain or commit the resources needed by the Stage Plan for the initiation stage
- Ensure that adequate reporting and control mechanisms are in place for the initiation stage
- Set tolerances for the initiation stage
- Request the necessary logistical support (for example accommodation, communication facilities, equipment and any Project Support) from corporate or programme management
- Understand any risks that affect the decision to authorize initiation
- Confirm to the Project Manager that the work defined in the Initiation Stage Plan may start.

Communicate:

- Keep stakeholders (corporate or programme management and other interested parties) informed about project progress by issuing a project initiation notification.

At this point, the Project Board is only authorizing the work of project initiation. The project as a whole is not being authorized. It is only the funding for the initiation stage that is being released to the Project Manager.

The Project Brief should be concise. Its purpose is to avoid time being wasted on detailed planning before there is adequate agreement on what the project is about and whether it is a worthwhile business investment. Some information may not be available, or agreed, at this early point. What is important is that sufficient information is agreed for the detailed planning to start.

4.3 INITIATING A PROJECT

4.3.1 Why is this important?

Once there is a decision to initiate a project, it needs to be planned in detail. Funding has to be obtained and controls defined to ensure that the project aligns with corporate strategy. The purpose of the Initiating a Project process is to establish solid foundations for the project, by scoping and

planning the project and expanding the Business Case. This will ensure that the Project Board has enough information to approve the overall project and authorize work on the first delivery stage.

If an organization proceeds directly from Starting up a Project to Controlling a Stage, it may be forced to commit significant financial resources to a project without fully understanding what it is or how its objectives will be achieved. Without this definition the Project Board will be taking a leap of faith.

4.3.2 Where does it fit and what happens?

This process involves:

- Defining the approach the project will take towards managing risks, quality, communication and control of the project's products
- Creating the Project Plan, showing the timescales and resources required for the project

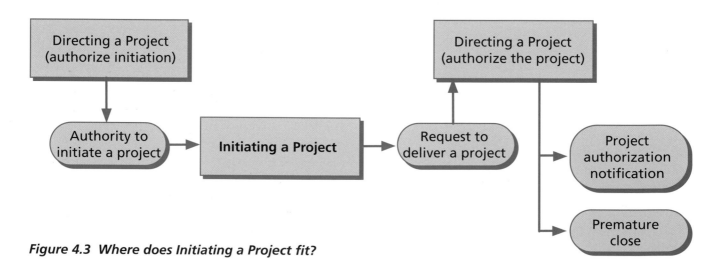

Figure 4.3 Where does Initiating a Project fit?

- Defining the scope of what is to be done and the products to be produced
- Refining the Project Brief into a detailed Business Case.

At the end of this process, the Project Manager requests authority from the Project Board to deliver the project. The Project Board reviews the information and will either authorize the project or order a premature close.

4.3.3 What is produced?

The initiation stage culminates in the production of the Project Initiation Documentation, which the Project Board reviews to decide whether to authorize the project.

Management products produced during this process include:

- **Project Initiation Documentation**   This is a refinement of the Project Brief, and includes the following main elements:
  - *Strategies*   These include the approach to be applied during the project to risk management, configuration management, quality management and communication management
  - *Summary of project controls*   These include the required frequency and format of communication between the project management levels, the number of stages, tolerances and the mechanisms to manage issues, changes and exceptions
  - *Project Plan*   This is a high-level view of the timescales and resource requirements for the whole project. It will include the product breakdown structure, product flow diagram and Product Descriptions for the major products to be produced by the project

- *Business Case*   This is a view of the project costs and potential benefits and risks. The Business Case is a key product and forms the basis of justifying the validity of the project
- **Registers**   These are created here and will be updated throughout the project with details of risks, issues and quality activities for the project. There are three registers:
  - *Risk Register*   This holds details of all risks facing the project and how they will be managed
  - *Issue Register*   This holds details of the issues being handled formally and provides a summary of all issues, their type, analysis and status
  - *Quality Register*   This holds the timings and resources for all quality activities planned to be conducted during the project
- **Benefits Review Plan**   This is a plan to show how and when each benefit included in the Business Case (some of which may only be achieved after the project is complete) is to be measured.

Example

The primary focus for the initiation stage for the UN Development Programme is to make sure a project has a solid mechanism for quality management and control. During this stage the Product Descriptions, Communication Strategy and Project Plan are prepared. The Risk Register and Issue Register are also updated. A central system enables capture of all plans, serving as a platform to manage the project and benchmark performance. The executive group, performing the Project Board role, will then approve the project to move to the next stage.

Table 4.2 outlines the roles which are responsible for completing the activities relevant to this process.

Table 4.2 Initiating a Project: roles

Role	Responsibility
Project Manager	Preparing the project strategies
	Setting up project controls
	Creating the Project Plan
	Refining the Business Case
	Assembling the Project Initiation Documentation

4.3.4 Directing a Project – authorize the project

This is triggered by a request from the Project Manager for authorization to proceed with the next stage. It should be performed in parallel to the activity to authorize a Stage Plan or Exception Plan, so that the overall project can be approved and work can be authorized to start on delivering the stage. The objective is to decide whether to proceed with the rest of the project. If the Project Board does not authorize the project, then it should be prematurely closed.

To authorize the project, the Project Board will collectively undertake the following responsibilities.

Actions required for authorizing the project

Approve the components of the Project Initiation Documentation:

- Confirm that the Business Case is viable, desirable and achievable and meets corporate or programme management expectations and standards. Approve the Business Case

- Confirm that lessons from previous similar projects have been reviewed and incorporated
- Confirm that the Quality Management Strategy will deliver the quality expectations, and approve it
- Confirm that the Configuration Management Strategy will deliver the approach expected, and approve it
- Confirm that the Risk Management Strategy will safeguard the project, and approve it
- Confirm that there has been a risk assessment, and that risk response actions are planned
- Confirm the validity and achievability of the Project Plan (and in particular the Project Board's commitment of the resources requested) and approve it
- Confirm that the Benefits Review Plan covers all expected benefits and approve it
- Confirm that all members of the project management team have agreed their roles (the project management team structure, roles and responsibilities)
- Ensure that the project controls are adequate for the nature of the project
- Ensure that the information needs and timing of communications, as defined in the Communication Management Strategy, are adequate for the nature of the project, and approve it
- Review the tolerances for the project provided by corporate or programme management

- Consider the consistency of the various components and approve the Project Initiation Documentation overall.

Communicate:

- Keep stakeholders (corporate or programme management and other interested parties) informed about project progress by issuing a project authorization notification.

4.4 CONTROLLING A STAGE/MANAGING PRODUCT DELIVERY

4.4.1 Why is this important?

Once the Project Board authorizes the delivery of a management stage, work to produce the products from that stage can start. The purpose of the Controlling a Stage process is to assign work to be done, monitor its progress, deal with issues, report progress to the Project Board and take corrective actions to ensure that the stage remains within tolerance.

This process allows the Project Manager to maintain control over the delivery of the project's products. From the Project Board's perspective, this process allows the members of the Project Board to practise management by exception, with the knowledge that they are being kept up to date with the project's progress.

It is closely related to the Managing Product Delivery process, where the project's specialist products are created.

4.4.2 Where does it fit and what happens?

Controlling a Stage is where the Project Manager conducts most of the day-to-day management of

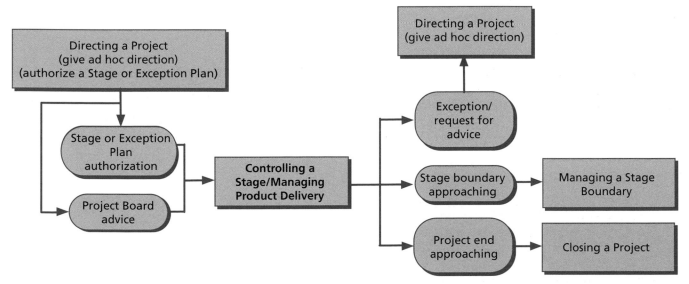

Figure 4.4 Where does Controlling a Stage/Managing Product Delivery fit?

the project. There are three main aspects to the process:

- Authorizing work, reviewing its progress and receiving completed work
- Reviewing the status of a stage and reporting progress to the Project Board
- Capturing and examining issues and risks, taking corrective action and requesting advice or escalating to the Project Board where necessary.

Managing Product Delivery is where the Team Manager(s) or team members execute assigned Work Packages (which will deliver one or more specialist products) and keep the Project Manager appraised of progress via regular reports.

4.4.3 What is produced?

Products produced by the Controlling a Stage and Managing Product Delivery processes include:

- **Work Package** This contains details of the work which is to be authorized by the Project Manager. It includes Product Descriptions for the products to be produced, and agreements on delivery dates, costs, tolerances and effort requirements. The focus is on getting negotiated agreement and clarity on what is to be produced, when and by whom. The Team Manager negotiates, accepts and executes the Work Package, and advises the Project Manager when it is complete
- **Highlight Report** The Project Manager produces regular Highlight Reports to keep the Project Board informed about the progress of a stage. These can be formal or informal
- **Exception Report** If a stage is forecast to exceed its tolerances, then the Project Manager will raise this to the Project Board through an

Exception Report, which provides reasons for the forecast deviation and options
- **Issue Report** This contains the description, impact assessment and recommendations for a Request for Change, off-specification or problem/concern. It is only created for those issues which need to be handled formally
- **Team Plan (if required)** The Team Manager produces this to show that the required products can be completed within the given constraints
- **Checkpoint Reports** The Team Manager reports progress to the Project Manager, at a frequency outlined in the Work Package
- **Specialist products** During the Managing Product Delivery process the Team Manager manages the production of the specialist products as outlined in the Work Package and Team Plan.

As the stage progresses, the Project Manager will also update the logs and registers, for example in response to any new risks, issues or quality activities which need to be managed, and the Stage Plan with details of progress and products completed.

Table 4.3 outlines the roles which are responsible for completing the activities relevant to the Controlling a Stage and Managing Product Delivery processes.

Example

For UN Development Programme projects, product delivery is managed through a set of contractual relationships with responsible parties, which could include private organizations, other United Nations organizations, government ministries, civil service organizations or non-governmental organizations. The Work Package is defined in a contract, a memorandum of understanding or a terms-of-reference document, which is signed and agreed between the organization managing the project and the contracted entity. Quality criteria, tolerances and schedules are outlined in these documents, and budgets, schedules and quality criteria are tracked in a central system. Typically, quarterly reviews are held to review progress against plans.

Table 4.3 Controlling a Stage/Managing Product Delivery: roles

Role	Responsibility
Project Manager	Authorizing a Work Package
	Reviewing Work Package status
	Receiving completed Work Packages
	Reviewing stage status
	Reporting highlights
	Capturing and examining issues and risks
	Escalating issues and risks
	Taking corrective action
Team Manager	Accepting, executing and delivering a Work Package

4.4.4 Directing a Project – give ad hoc direction

An important aspect of the Project Board's role is to provide formal or informal guidance at any time during the project, as a result of requests, reports, external influences, input from corporate or programme management, Exception Reports or escalated Issue Reports. As the Project Manager manages the project on behalf of the Project Board, it is important that Project Board members make time available for the Project Manager if required.

To give ad hoc direction, the Project Board will collectively and individually undertake the following responsibilities.

Actions required for giving ad hoc direction

Respond to requests:

- Review the request. This could be informal or formal (in the form of an Issue Report)
- Make a decision – approve, reject, defer decision, request more information
- Provide guidance to the Project Manager.

Respond to reports:

- Review the latest Highlight Report to understand the status of the project
- Be satisfied, through dialogue with the Project Manager, that the stage is progressing according to plan
- Make decisions on Exception Reports – adjust tolerances or approve responses to the exception as appropriate.

Respond to external influences:

- Ensure that the project is kept informed of external events that may affect it
- Ensure that the project remains focused on the corporate or programme objectives set and remains justified in business terms
- Ensure that the Project Manager is notified of any changes in the corporate or programme environment that may impact on the project and that appropriate action is taken
- Where the project is part of a programme, if there is to be a change in the composition of the Project Board, the advice and approval of programme management should be sought.

Communicate:

- Advise the Project Manager of any change to Project Board personnel
- Keep stakeholders (corporate or programme management and other interested parties) informed about project progress, as defined by the Communication Management Strategy.

4.5 MANAGING A STAGE BOUNDARY

4.5.1 Why is this important?

The Project Board authorizes work on a stage-by-stage basis. Towards the end of each management stage, the Project Manager will request authorization to proceed to the next stage. The purpose of the Managing a Stage Boundary process is to provide the Project Board with enough information so that it can confirm that the project continues to align with the organization's needs and that the Business Case remains viable. The same process is used to provide the Project Board with sufficient information to approve an Exception Plan, if this is required to replace the Project Plan or current Stage Plan.

The benefit of using a staged approach to a project is that the Project Board will review the project at specific times and only approve its continuation if it remains viable. If the business justification for the project no longer exists, the Project Board can change or stop the project.

4.5.2 Where does it fit and what happens?

The main activities during this process include:

- Updating the Project Plan and the Business Case with actual results from the stage
- Planning the next stage in detail or producing an Exception Plan, if this has been requested by the Project Board
- Producing an End Stage Report outlining the progress achieved during the stage.

4.5.3 What is produced?

Management products produced during this process include:

- **Stage Plan or Exception Plan** Showing the products (including Product Descriptions), activities, timeframes and resources for the next management stage
- **End Stage Report** The Project Manager produces a summary of the progress to date and the overall project situation, and provides the Project Board with sufficient information to approve or reject the next stage
- **Project Plan and Business Case** The Project Manager updates these to show the actual progress from the stage that is finishing, to include the forecast duration and costs from the next Stage Plan or Exception Plan and to show any revised costs.

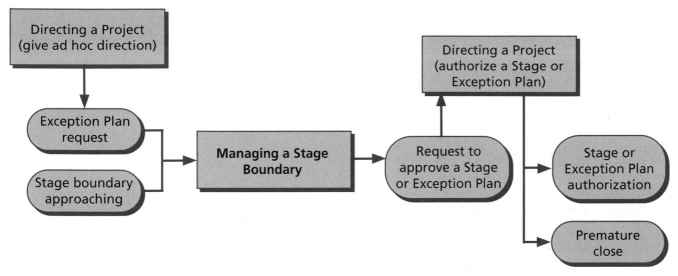

Figure 4.5 Where does Managing a Stage Boundary fit?

The Project Manager will also keep the project records up to date with actual results from the stage. Table 4.4 outlines the roles which are responsible for completing the activities relevant to the Managing a Stage Boundary process.

Table 4.4 Managing a Stage Boundary: roles

Role	Responsibility
Project Manager	Producing the next Stage Plan or Exception Plan
	Updating the Project Plan and Business Case
	Reporting stage end

4.5.4 Directing a Project – authorize a Stage Plan or Exception Plan

It is important that a stage starts only when the Project Board says it should. The Project Board authorizes a management stage by reviewing the performance of the current stage and approving the Stage Plan for the next stage. If an exception has occurred during the stage, the Project Board may request that the Project Manager produces an Exception Plan for Project Board approval. If the Project Board does not authorize the Stage Plan or Exception Plan, then the project should be prematurely terminated.

To authorize a Stage or Exception Plan, the Project Board will collectively undertake the following responsibilities.

Actions required for authorizing a Stage or Exception Plan

Review the End Stage Report (or Exception Report):

- If this is the end of a management stage, then review the performance status of the project using the End Stage Report for the current management stage. Include consideration of any benefits achieved or lessons learned during the stage
- If there is an exception, then review the status of the project and the background to the exception using the Exception Report.

Review and approve the next Stage Plan or Exception Plan:

- Review the plan for which the Project Manager is seeking approval (this will be a Stage Plan for the next management stage or an Exception Plan)
- Set the tolerances for the next management stage or (in the case of an Exception Plan) revise the current stage tolerances if necessary.

Assess overall project viability:

- Review the Project Plan and the position in relation to project tolerances agreed with corporate or programme management
- Review the Business Case to ensure that the project is still justified
- Review the key risks to ensure that the exposure is still acceptable and that response actions are planned
- Obtain decisions from outside the project for any potential deviations beyond project tolerances. For example, if this project is part

of a programme, programme management will have to examine the likely impact on the programme and take appropriate action

- Authorize the Project Manager to proceed with the submitted plan (Stage Plan or Exception Plan) or instruct the Project Manager to prematurely close the project.

Communicate:

- Inform stakeholders (corporate or programme management and other interested parties) on project progress.

4.6   CLOSING A PROJECT

4.6.1 Why is this important?

During the final delivery stage (once the Project Manager has gained approval for all the project's products) it is time to decommission the project. The purpose of this process is to provide a fixed point at which acceptance for the project's products is confirmed and to recognize either that objectives set out in the original Project Initiation Documentation have been achieved (or approved changes to the objectives have been achieved), or that the project has nothing more to contribute.

4.6.2 Where does it fit and what happens?

The Project Board needs to be satisfied that the recipients of the project's products can own and use them on an ongoing basis. The products can then be transitioned into operational use and the project can close. The project documentation should be tidied up and archived, the project assessed for performance against its original plan and the resources assigned to the project released. The closure activities include planning post-project benefits reviews to take place for those benefits that can only be assessed after the products have been in use (and therefore after the project has closed).

4.6.3 What is produced?

Management products produced during this stage include:

- **End Project Report** This reviews the success of the project compared with the Project Initiation Documentation and details any recommendations for follow-on actions to be conducted after project closure
- **Lessons Report** This includes any recommendations for improvements to processes which may apply to future projects.

Products are handed over to the relevant operations and maintenance organizations for ongoing support. The Project Manager also closes the project records such as the registers and logs, and produces a recommendation, for submission to the Project Board, to give notice to corporate or programme management that project resources are about to be released.

Table 4.5 outlines the roles which are responsible for completing the activities relevant to this process.

Table 4.5 Closing a Project: roles

Role	Responsibility
Project Manager	Preparing planned or premature closure
	Handing over products
	Evaluating the project
	Recommending project closure

4.6.4 Directing a Project – authorize project closure

The Project Board reviews the Project Initiation Documentation and the Project Plan to assess whether the objectives of the project were achieved and the project can be closed, and communicates the closure of the project to

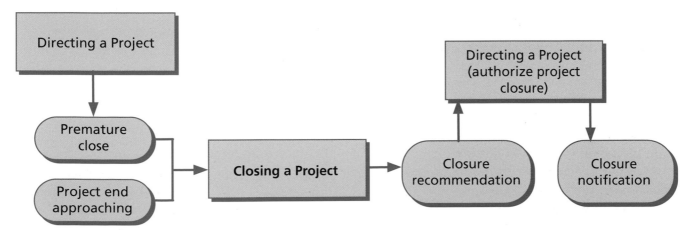

Figure 4.6 Where does Closing a Project fit?

Examples

United Nations

For the UN Development Programme, closing a project involves operational closure (all activities complete and all project outputs achieved), followed by financial closure (all financial transactions complete and all accounts closed). As part of project closure, follow-on actions and guidance notes are documented to support the future evaluation of the programme within which the project resides. These notes could include, for example, suggested timings for tracking of project benefits realization or suggestions for follow-on projects. A final project review report articulates results achieved and lessons learned.

Australian government

PRINCE2 guidelines for items to consider when documenting lessons have proved to be beneficial to the Department of Families, Housing, Community Services and Indigenous Affairs, an Australian federal government department. At the conclusion of a complex project involving the development of a new information system, the Project Manager used the suggested composition for a Lessons Report, and this helped to identify a comprehensive range of lessons learned during the project. The Project Board formally approved the Lessons Report at project closure, and it was widely distributed within the organization and presented to other Project Managers at a regular review meeting. This not only ensured that corporate knowledge was captured but also that it was then able to be shared and used effectively by other Project Managers.

corporate or programme management. Without this approach, the project may never end – it can become 'business as usual' and the original focus on business benefits will be lost. This is the last project activity, and its purpose is to confirm an orderly close of the project before the project team is finally disbanded. The Project Board needs to be confident that the products of the project work have been handed over and accepted by the functions responsible for using and maintaining them, that the nature and ownership of any follow-on action has been agreed, that measures are in place to realize the benefits from the project, and that the participating organizations exploit any lessons learned.

To authorize project closure, the Project Board will collectively undertake the following responsibilities.

Actions required for authorizing project closure

Confirm handover and acceptance:

- Verify that the handover of the project product was in accordance with the Configuration Management Strategy and in particular that records of all required user acceptance and operational/maintenance acceptance exist
- Ensure that, where appropriate, the resulting changes in the business are supported and sustainable
- Ensure that any customer quality expectations that cannot be validated until after the project closes (e.g. performance levels regarding reliability) are included in the Benefits Review Plan as a post-project check.

Approve the End Project Report:

- The version of the Project Initiation Documentation which was approved at project initiation should be used as the baseline to assess how the project has deviated from its initial basis, and to provide information against which the success of the project can be judged
- Ensure follow-on action recommendations have been recorded correctly in the End Project Report and that the appropriate groups have been made aware of their responsibility for taking them forward
- Approve the End Project Report for distribution to stakeholders, for example corporate or programme management
- Review the Lessons Report and agree who should receive it. Ensure that the appropriate groups (for example corporate or programme management, or a centre of excellence) have been made aware of their responsibility for taking any recommendations forward.

Confirm the Business Case:

- Confirm the updated Business Case by comparing actual and forecast benefits, costs and risks against the Business Case approved with the Project Initiation Documentation (it may not be possible to validate all the benefits as some will not be realized until after the project is closed).

Approve the Benefits Review Plan:

- Review and gain approval for the updated Benefits Review Plan, ensuring that it addresses the expected benefits that cannot yet be validated

- As the Benefits Review Plan includes resources beyond the life of the project, responsibility for this plan needs to transfer to corporate or programme management.

Issue the project closure notification:

- Review and issue a project closure notification in accordance with the Communication Management Strategy
- Advise those who have provided the support infrastructure and resources for the project that these can now be withdrawn
- Release the resources provided to the project
- Provide a closing date for costs being charged to the project.

Project Board duties and behaviours

5

5 Project Board duties and behaviours

5.1 THE ROLE OF SENIOR MANAGEMENT IN PRINCE2

Project Board members represent the most senior level of management in the PRINCE2 project management team. They can rarely afford to get involved in the detail of every project for which they are responsible. It is crucial that they can delegate project work effectively.

In PRINCE2, the Project Board delegates the management of the project to the Project Manager in a series of stages, each based on an approved Stage Plan. Provided the Project Manager can deliver the stage within the tolerances defined in the Stage Plan, Project Board members do not need to maintain close contacts with the work and can manage by exception. The stage boundaries represent major control milestones, when the Project Board reviews whether the Project Manager has delivered the previous stage and approves a plan for the next stage.

Senior managers acting as Project Board members must also provide leadership and direction to ensure that their projects remain aligned to the organization's strategic aims. If the composition of the Project Board is deficient then the project is likely to struggle. If the Project Board is embroiled in in-fighting the project is almost certainly doomed. Appointing the right Project Board is probably the single most important factor in achieving a successful project.

The duties of the Project Board are to:

- Be accountable for the project
- Provide unified direction
- Delegate effectively
- Facilitate cross-functional integration
- Commit resources
- Ensure effective decision making
- Support the Project Manager
- Ensure effective communication.

5.2 BE ACCOUNTABLE FOR THE PROJECT

The Project Board is accountable for the success (or failure) of the project.

The Project Board is accountable to corporate or programme management for the success or failure of the project within the constraints defined in the project mandate. Being accountable means accepting and demonstrating ownership of the project. The Executive is seen as the focus of accountability for the project, and this role retains the ultimate decision-making authority. However, projects require the interests of all three stakeholder categories (business, user and supplier) to be satisfied in order to be successful. This means that there is an obligation on the Senior User and Senior Supplier to ensure that the interests of their respective areas are safeguarded.

For instance, the Senior User role is accountable for ensuring that the products of the project will enable the intended benefits to be realized operationally. If this does not happen the project may be considered 'successfully' completed but the business benefits may never be realized.

The Senior Supplier role is accountable for ensuring that the products of the project are reliable, properly integrated, can be maintained efficiently etc. If this does not happen, the later stages of the project are likely to be fraught with problems, with repeated failures of the intended solution – or benefits might be offset by operational maintenance difficulties after project closure.

Also, given that the Executive has the ultimate decision-making authority, it is important that the Executive has the requisite level of authority in practice. If other Project Board members are more senior in the host organization it may prove difficult for the Executive to manage their contributions effectively.

5.3 PROVIDE UNIFIED DIRECTION

Project Board members must provide unified direction.

Unified direction is about teamwork at Project Board level. While each Project Board member has accountability for satisfying the interests of a particular stakeholder category (business, user or supplier), it is crucial that all members agree on the overall direction for the project.

This can involve compromises. Frequently the 'best' solution to a problem cannot be determined by objective evaluation, but is simply the one that Project Board members can agree on. Users may favour a project approach or solution that suppliers consider inappropriate – perhaps because it is incompatible with an established strategy/ standard, or expensive to support. Project Board members need to resolve these issues, focusing on the likely impact on business benefits, and communicate the outcome in a way that minimizes any potential for friction.

Example

In an internal IT project for an international company based in New York, the Senior Supplier was perceived as having more influence in the company than the non-IT project Executive. The Senior Supplier was a long-serving senior manager with a lot of experience and a network of contacts – whereas the Executive was a relatively young manager, recently appointed as manager of the overall programme.

The Executive and the Senior Supplier differed over aspects of the international IT strategy agreed for the overall programme. The Senior Supplier had sufficient business influence to be able to resist its implementation on the project concerned, which was at the core of the programme. The disagreement at Project Board level caused uncertainty and delays in the project work. Irrespective of the rights and wrongs in the debate about strategy, the problem was that decision making was disrupted and decisions were evaded because of internal politics – which the project Executive was not sufficiently senior to resolve.

Eventually, corporate management became impatient with the lack of momentum and the result was that the entire Project Board and the senior programme management team were replaced.

5.4 DELEGATE EFFECTIVELY

Project Board members must delegate effectively, using the PRINCE2 organizational structure and controls designed for this purpose.

Several aspects of PRINCE2 are designed to promote effective delegation, for example:

■ A clearly defined framework of roles and responsibilities in the project organization
■ Plans designed to meet the needs of managers at different levels
■ The use of management stages for planning and progress control.

The Stage Plan can be viewed as a 'notional contract' between the Project Board and the Project Manager, as outlined in the box below.

The stage contract

The Project Board undertakes, collectively, to:

■ Provide overall direction
■ Commit the resources in the plan.

The Project Manager undertakes, subject to approved tolerances, to:

■ Deliver the stage products
■ Meet the product quality criteria
■ Deliver within the stage budget
■ Meet the target completion date.

The Project Board uses Highlight Reports to confirm that the stage remains on track, and can use Project Assurance to confirm that their various stakeholder interests are safeguarded. With these arrangements, the PRINCE2 project proceeds to completion as a series of stage contracts, minimizing the formal participation required of the Project Board.

Stage tolerances provide a defined area of discretion within which the Project Manager can be left to manage. If the Project Manager forecasts that the stage cannot be completed within the agreed tolerances, an exception must be escalated to the Project Board. When an exception does occur, the Project Manager escalates by generating an Exception Report. This alerts Project Board members to the situation, outlines any different responses that are available and, if possible, recommends a way forward. Once this has been agreed, the Project Manager may be asked to produce an Exception Plan.

Project Board members may be the first to recognize an exception, for instance when changes arise in the wider programme or business environment that will impact the project. In this context, it is the responsibility of the Project Board to alert the Project Manager, but the exception planning approach is otherwise the same.

If an exception relates to project-level tolerances, the Project Board needs to escalate to corporate or programme management as it means that the project is forecast to go beyond the authority given to the Project Board.

5.5 FACILITATE CROSS-FUNCTIONAL INTEGRATION

The project management team is a temporary, almost always cross-functional, structure set up with specific responsibility for the project. Project Board members must ensure that this is recognized and respected in the functional or line management organization(s), and that the Project Board's authority is not undermined.

Projects do not happen in a vacuum. They are conducted as part of a wider corporate environment and involve a team of people with different skills working together (on a temporary basis) to introduce a change which will impact others outside the team. Projects often cross the normal functional divisions within an organization and sometimes span entirely different organizations. This frequently causes stresses and strains within organizations and between, for example, customers and suppliers.

The cross-functional characteristic of projects is one of the main reasons that project work is inherently more risky than 'business as usual' activity. An important part of the Project Board's role is to make sure that the project works effectively and is supported in the wider organization.

5.6   COMMIT RESOURCES

> Project Board members are responsible for committing the resources necessary for the successful completion of the project.

Project Board members should be able to deliver all the resources required for the success of the project.

The Project Manager is responsible for assembling the plans, and for identifying, communicating and agreeing the resource requirements. The Project Board must approve the plan for the work to commence. It is important that Project Board members understand that by approving a Project Plan or Stage Plan, they are endorsing it as a realistic plan and undertaking to commit the resources required. Project Board members cannot

subsequently distance themselves and blame the planners.

However, many factors can disrupt the process:

- It may not be possible to agree a resource plan that allows the project to meet other constraints, for example budget or schedule
- Resources that have been agreed may, in the event, become unavailable
- Project delays or other changes may alter the timing of resource requirements with the result that they cannot be met
- Where personnel are committed part-time, project work may be interrupted by competing 'business as usual' activity or contributions on other, higher-priority projects.

Many of these problems arise from competing business or line management priorities, and Project Board members must resolve any conflicts stemming from where the project fits in relation to the competing priorities.

Resourcing issues are typically the ones most frequently escalated to Project Board members. Where Project Board members fail to provide adequate support, resources may be deployed on the basis of whoever shouts loudest, resulting in unnecessary antagonism and at the expense of rational business decision making.

5.7   ENSURE EFFECTIVE DECISION MAKING

> Project Board members must ensure effective decision making.

A large part of the Project Board's role is to control progress on the project. The Project Board approves the Project Plan and Stage Plans, and assesses progress at Project Board reviews, the main ones being at stage boundaries. Project Board reviews are all based on essentially the same simple agenda, shown in the box below. The reviews should always focus on plans, approving them and assessing progress in relation to them.

A typical project board agenda

1 Look back

Review status in relation to the current Stage Plan (or Exception Plan)

2 Look forward

Preview the next Stage (or Exception) Plan

3 Assess overall project viability

Considering the current status of the Business Case, Project Plan and risks

4 Make a decision

Authorization to proceed by approving the next Stage Plan (or Exception Plan)?

The Project Board makes decisions on **risks, issues, changes** and **exceptions,** and may delegate decisions on off-specifications or requests for change to a separate Change Authority. The roles which will be responsible for making decisions on different categories of risks, issues and changes should be agreed when initiating the project and documented in the Project Initiation Documentation.

When progress and/or change issues result in an exception, the Project Board will either approve or reject an Exception Plan. The generic agenda outlined in the box above also applies to Project Board reviews prompted by exceptions.

The Project Board makes decisions on **quality** by approving:

- The Project Product Description, including the customer's quality expectations and acceptance criteria
- The Quality Management Strategy, including key quality responsibilities
- Product Descriptions.

Project Board members can ensure that their decisions are well-informed by delegating the tasks of monitoring the business, user and supplier interests to Project Assurance. Project Assurance can be implemented in a variety of different forms, for example with part-time or full-time personnel or with occasional, independent project health checks. It is an opportunity to make the right people and the right information available for decision making.

5.8 SUPPORT THE PROJECT MANAGER

Project Board members must provide effective support for the Project Manager.

The Project Manager is the focus for the day-to-day management of the project work and this is often a busy and stressful role. The Project Board can relieve some of this stress by demonstrating visible and sustained support for the Project Manager.

The Project Board can provide support to the Project Manager in many different ways. Communicating and reinforcing the fact that the Project Manager has the Project Board's delegated authority, ensuring that resources committed in plans are actually delivered, providing adequate Project Support to the project and allowing sufficient time for planning will all contribute towards easing the Project Manager role. Being readily accessible to provide advice and guidance where needed and responding promptly when issues are escalated will also help.

5.9 ENSURE EFFECTIVE COMMUNICATION

The Project Board must ensure that communication is timely and effective, both within the project and with the key external stakeholders.

The Project Board is the channel for communication between the project and external stakeholders. The Communication Management Strategy contains the frequency and types of communication required for the project.

Important aspects to consider are:

■ Who are the audiences for project communication, and how will the project impact them?
■ What communication channels should be used?
■ What are the key messages?
■ When is communication needed?

Project Board members are responsible for communicating effectively with corporate or programme management sponsoring the project. Perceptions at that level are crucial to continuing business visibility and support.

Tailoring PRINCE2 to the project environment

6

6 Tailoring PRINCE2 to the project environment

The 'tailoring' principle states that PRINCE2 must be tailored to suit the project's environment, size, complexity, importance, capability and risk. The purpose of tailoring is to ensure that the project management method aligns to business processes such as human resources, finance and procurement, and also that the project controls, such as the frequency and formality of reporting, are appropriate for the project.

Tailoring refers to the appropriate use of PRINCE2 on any given project, ensuring that there is the correct amount of planning, control, governance and use of the processes and themes, whereas the adoption of PRINCE2 across an organization is known as **embedding**. Table 6.1 sets out the difference between embedding and tailoring.

Tailoring does not consist of omitting elements of PRINCE2. It is about adapting the method to external factors (such as any corporate standards that need to be applied) and the project factors to consider (such as the scale of the project). The goal is to apply a level of project management that does not overburden the project but provides an appropriate level of control given the external and project factors.

The danger of not tailoring PRINCE2 is that it can lead to 'robotic' project management if every process activity is followed and every management product is produced without question. Figure 6.1

Table 6.1 Embedding and tailoring

Embedding (done by the organization to adopt PRINCE2)	Tailoring (done by the project management team to adapt the method to the context of a specific project)
Focus on: ■ Process responsibilities ■ Scaling rules/guidance (e.g. score card) ■ Standards (templates, definitions) ■ Training and development ■ Integration with business processes ■ Tools ■ Process assurance.	Focus on: ■ Adapting the themes (through the strategies and controls) ■ Incorporating specific terms/language ■ Revising the Product Descriptions for the management products ■ Revising the role descriptions for the PRINCE2 project roles ■ Adjusting the processes to match the above.
Guidance in PRINCE2 Maturity Model (P2MM)	Guidance in *Managing Successful Projects with PRINCE2* (TSO, 2009)

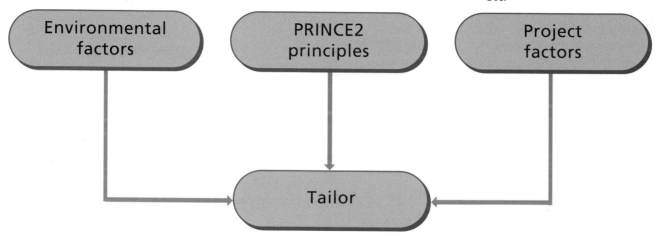

- Multi-organization
- External customer/supplier
- Corporate standards
- Within a programme
- Organization maturity
  (e.g. centre of excellence)
- Terms and language
- Geography
- Organization culture
- Project priority
- etc.

- Scale
- Solution complexity
- Team maturity
- Project type and lifecycle model
- etc.

Environmental factors

PRINCE2 principles

Project factors

Tailor

- Adapt the themes (through the strategies and controls)
- Revise terms and language
- Revise Product Descriptions for the management products
- Revise role descriptions
- Adjust processes to match the above
- Record in the Project Initiation Documentation

Figure 6.1 Influences on the tailoring requirement

shows some of the environmental and project factors involved in tailoring.

Tailoring PRINCE2 involves:

- **Applying the principles** As these are universal they will apply to every project and are not tailored

- **Adapting the themes** Including relevant corporate or programme standards in the project's management products

- **Applying the organization's terms and language** For instance, if the host organization uses the term 'phases' rather than 'stages' it may be appropriate to substitute the term for the project's documentation

- **Adapting the management products** Modifying the Product Descriptions for the management products used
- **Adapting the roles** Adapting the standard role descriptions to the context of the project
- **Adapting the processes** Defining the responsibilities for performing activities or references to management products, if these have been changed.

6.1 TAILORING PRINCE2 FOR PROJECTS IN A PROGRAMME ENVIRONMENT

One specific situation where PRINCE2 must be tailored is when a project is run as part of a larger programme.

> A **programme** is a temporary flexible organization structure created to coordinate, direct and oversee the implementation of a set of related projects and activities in order to deliver outcomes and benefits relating to an organization's strategic objectives. A programme may have a life that spans several years.

A programme organization tends to have a lifespan that includes the realization of benefits – unlike projects, where the benefits are usually accrued after the project has been disbanded. When projects are run as part of a programme, PRINCE2 will need to be tailored to meet the needs of the programme environment.

Example

When a project is part of a programme, the project **Business Case** may be aggregated into the programme Business Case and therefore may not be as detailed as for a stand-alone project. The programme may also produce and maintain the Business Case, and programme management will define, track and manage the benefits.

The **organization** structures at programme and project level should be integrated to ensure clear lines of responsibility and reduce duplication, for example allocating the Programme Manager to the role of Executive for one or more projects.

The **Starting up a Project** process could be undertaken at programme level, with the programme appointing the Executive and Project Manager, reviewing previous lessons, appointing the project management team and preparing the Project Brief.

The project **logs** and **registers** could be maintained either at the project or programme level – for instance, there may be a separate Risk Register for each project in a programme, or a single one which covers all risks for the programme.

6.2 TAILORING PRINCE2 ACCORDING TO PROJECT SCALE

Projects can vary in size and complexity from small and simple to a large, risky or complex, and this scale will affect how PRINCE2 should be tailored. Table 6.2 shows an approach to categorizing projects and how PRINCE2 can be tailored according to the scale of the project.

Appendix A: Product Description outlines

A

Appendix A: Product Description outlines

PRINCE2 defines a set of management products that will be required as part of managing the project and establishing and maintaining quality. Management products are not necessarily documents – they are information sets used by the PRINCE2 processes so that certain roles can take action and/or make decisions.

There are three types of management product: baselines, records and reports. Baseline management products are those that define aspects of the project and, once approved, are subject to change control. Records are dynamic management products that maintain information regarding project progress. Reports are management products which provide a snapshot of the status of certain aspects of the project.

This section contains Product Description outlines taken from the main volume, *Managing Successful Projects with PRINCE2* (TSO, 2009), for selected baseline management products and reports. These outlines are summarized and do not include all of the headings and content of a Product Description. The contents of a Product Description for a management product should be tailored to the requirements and environment of each project. Note that the numbering system in this appendix reflects the system used in the main volume, and because certain management products and/or subsections may not be included, the numbered headings given here are not always sequential.

A.1 BENEFITS REVIEW PLAN

A.1.1 Purpose
A Benefits Review Plan is used to define how and when a measurement of the achievement of the project's benefits can be made. It is used during the Closing a Project process to define any post-project benefits reviews that are required.

A.1.2 Composition
- The scope of the Benefits Review Plan covering what benefits are to be measured
- Who is accountable for the expected benefits
- How to measure achievement of expected benefits, and when they can be measured
- What resources are needed to carry out the review work
- Baseline measures from which the improvements will be calculated.

A.2 BUSINESS CASE

A.2.1 Purpose
A Business Case is used to document the justification for the undertaking of a project, based on the estimated costs (of development, implementation and incremental ongoing operations and maintenance costs) against the anticipated benefits to be gained and offset by any associated risks.

The Project Board will monitor the ongoing viability of the project against the Business Case.

A.2.2 Composition

- **Executive summary** Highlights the key points in the Business Case, which should include important benefits and the return on investment (ROI)
- **Reasons** Defines the reasons for undertaking the project and explains how the project will enable the achievement of corporate strategies and objectives
- **Business options** Analysis and reasoned recommendation for the base business options of: do nothing, do the minimal or do something
- **Expected benefits** The benefits that the project will deliver expressed in measurable terms against the situation as it exists prior to the project. Tolerances should be set for each benefit and for the aggregated benefit
- **Expected dis-benefits** Outcomes perceived as negative by one or more stakeholders. Dis-benefits need to be valued and incorporated into the investment appraisal
- **Timescale** Over which the project will run (summary of the Project Plan) and the period over which the benefits will be realized
- **Costs** A summary of the project costs (taken from the Project Plan), the ongoing operations and maintenance costs and their funding arrangements
- **Investment appraisal** Compares the aggregated benefits and dis-benefits to the project costs (extracted from the Project Plan) and ongoing incremental operations and maintenance costs. The objective is to be able to define the value of a project as an investment. The investment appraisal should address how the project will be funded

- **Major risks** Gives a summary of the key risks associated with the project together with the likely impact and plans should they occur.

A.3 CHECKPOINT REPORT

A.3.1 Purpose

A Checkpoint Report is used to report, at a frequency defined in the Work Package, the status of the Work Package.

A.3.2 Composition

- **Date** The date of the checkpoint
- **Period** The reporting period covered by the Checkpoint Report
- **Follow-ups** From previous reports, for example action items completed or issues outstanding
- **This reporting period:**
  - The products being developed by the team during the reporting period
  - The products completed by the team during the reporting period
  - Quality management activities carried out during the period
  - Lessons identified
- **Next reporting period:**
  - The products being developed by the team in the next reporting period
  - The products planned to be completed by the team in the next reporting period
  - Quality management activities planned for the next reporting period
- **Work Package tolerance status** How execution of the Work Package is performing against its tolerances (e.g. cost/time/scope actuals and forecast)

■ **Issues and risks** Update on issues and risks associated with the Work Package.

A.8 END PROJECT REPORT

A.8.1 Purpose

An End Project Report is used during project closure to review how the project performed against the version of the Project Initiation Documentation used to authorize it.

A.8.2 Composition

■ **Project Manager's report** Summarizing the project's performance

■ **Review of the Business Case** Summarizing the validity of the project's Business Case

■ **Review of project objectives** Review of how the project performed against its planned targets and tolerances for time, cost, quality, scope, benefits and risk

■ **Review of team performance** In particular, providing recognition for good performance

■ **Review of products** Including quality activities, approval records, off-specifications, handover of the project product, and summary of follow-on action recommendations

■ **Lessons Report** (see section A.15) A review of what went well, what went badly, and any recommendations for corporate or programme management consideration.

A.9 END STAGE REPORT

A.9.1 Purpose

An End Stage Report is used to give a summary of progress to date, the overall project situation, and sufficient information to ask for a Project Board decision on what to do next with the project.

A.9.2 Composition

■ **Project Manager's report** Summarizing the stage performance

■ **Review of the Business Case** Summarizing the validity of the project's Business Case

■ **Review of project objectives** Review of how the project has performed to date against its planned targets and tolerances for time, cost, quality, scope, benefits and risk

■ **Review of stage objectives** Review of how the specific stage performed against its planned targets and tolerances for time, cost, quality, scope, benefits and risk

■ **Review of team performance** In particular, providing recognition for good performance

■ **Review of products:** Including quality records, approval records, off-specifications, phased handover (if applicable) and summary of follow-on action recommendations (if applicable)

■ **Lessons Report** (if appropriate) (see section A.15) A review of what went well, what went badly, and any recommendations for corporate or programme management consideration

■ **Issues and risks** Summary of the current set of issues and risks affecting the project

■ **Forecast** The Project Manager's forecast for the project and next stage against planned targets and tolerances for time, cost, quality, scope, benefits and risk.

A.10 EXCEPTION REPORT

A.10.1 Purpose

An Exception Report is produced when a Stage Plan or Project Plan is forecast to exceed tolerance levels set. It is prepared by the Project Manager in order to inform the Project Board of the situation, and to offer options and recommendations for the way to proceed.

A.10.2 Composition

■ **Exception title**   An overview of the exception being reported
■ **Cause of the exception**   A description of the cause of a deviation from the current plan
■ **Consequences of the deviation**   What the implications are if the deviation is not addressed
■ **Options**   What are the options that are available to address the deviation and what would the effect of each option be on the Business Case, risks and tolerances
■ **Recommendation**   Of the available options, what is the recommendation, and why?
■ **Lessons**   What can be learned from the exception, on this project or future projects.

A.11 HIGHLIGHT REPORT

A.11.1 Purpose

A Highlight Report is used to provide the Project Board (and possibly other stakeholders) with a summary of the stage status at intervals defined by them. The Project Board uses the report to monitor stage and project progress. The Project Manager also uses it to advise the Project Board of any potential problems or areas where the Project Board could help.

A.11.2 Composition

■ **Date**   The date of the report
■ **Period**   The reporting period covered by the Highlight Report
■ **Status summary**   An overview of the status of the stage at this time
■ **This reporting period:**
  ● Work Packages – pending authorization, in execution, and completed in the period
  ● Products completed in the period
  ● Products planned but not started or completed in the period
  ● Corrective actions taken during the period
■ **Next reporting period:**
  ● Work Packages – to be authorized, in execution, and to be completed during the next period
  ● Products to be completed in the next period
  ● Corrective actions to be completed during the next period
■ **Project and stage tolerance status**   How execution of the project and stage are performing against their tolerances (e.g. cost/ time actuals and forecast)
■ **Requests for change**   Raised, approved/rejected and pending
■ **Key issues and risks**   Summary of actual or potential problems and risks
■ **Lessons Report** (if appropriate) (see section A.15)   A review of what went well, what went badly, and any recommendations for corporate or programme management consideration.

A.13   ISSUE REPORT

A.13.1 Purpose

An Issue Report is a report containing the description, impact assessment and recommendations for a request for change, off-specification or a problem/concern. It is only created for those issues that need to be handled formally.

A.13.2 Composition

- **Issue identifier**   As shown in the Issue Register (provides a unique reference for every Issue Report)
- **Issue type**   Defines the type of issue being recorded, namely:
  - Request for change
  - Off-specification
  - Problem/concern
- **Date raised**   The date on which the issue was originally raised
- **Raised by**   The name of the individual or team who raised the issue
- **Issue Report author**   The name of the individual or team who created the Issue Report
- **Issue description**   A statement describing the issue in terms of its cause and impact
- **Impact analysis**   A detailed analysis of the likely impact of the issue. This may include, for example, a list of products impacted
- **Recommendation**   A description of what the Project Manager believes should be done to resolve the issue (and why)
- **Priority**   This should be given in terms of the project's chosen scale. It should be re-evaluated after impact analysis

- **Severity**   This should be given in terms of the project's chosen scale. Severity will indicate what level of management is required to make a decision on the issue
- **Decision**   The decision made (accept, reject, defer or grant concession)
- **Approved by**   A record of who made the decision
- **Decision date**   The date of the decision
- **Closure date**   The date that the issue was closed.

A.15   LESSONS REPORT

A.15.1 Purpose

The Lessons Report is used to pass on any lessons that can be usefully applied to other projects.

The data in the report should be used by the corporate group that is responsible for the quality management system, in order to refine, change and improve the standards. Statistics on how much effort was needed for products can help improve future estimating.

A.15.2 Composition

- Executive summary
- Scope of the report (e.g. stage or project)
- A review of what went well, what went badly and any recommendations for corporate or programme management consideration. In particular:
  - Project management method (including the tailoring of PRINCE2)
  - Any specialist methods used
  - Project strategies (risk management, quality management, communications management and configuration management)

- Project controls (and the effectiveness of any tailoring)
- Abnormal events causing deviations
■ A review of useful measurements.

A.16 PLAN

A.16.1 Purpose

A plan provides a statement of how and when objectives are to be achieved, by showing the major products, activities and resources required for the scope of the plan. In PRINCE2, there are three levels of plan: project, stage and team. An Exception Plan is created at the same level as the plan that it is replacing.

A.16.2 Composition

■ **Plan description**   Covering a brief description of what the plan encompasses (i.e. project, stage, team, exception) and the planning approach
■ **Plan prerequisites**   Containing any fundamental aspects that must be in place, and remain in place, for the plan to succeed
■ **External dependencies**   That may influence the plan
■ **Planning assumptions**   Upon which the plan is based
■ **Lessons incorporated**   Details of relevant lessons from previous similar projects, which have been reviewed and accommodated within this plan
■ **Monitoring and control**   Details of how the plan will be monitored and controlled
■ **Budgets**   Covering time and cost, including provisions for risks and changes

■ **Tolerances**   Time, cost and scope tolerances for the level of plan (which may also include more specific stage- or team-level risk tolerances)
■ **Product Descriptions** (see section A.17) Covering the products within the scope of the plan
■ **Schedule**   Which may include graphical representations of:
  - Gantt or bar chart
  - Product breakdown structure
  - Product flow diagram
  - Activity network
  - Table of resource requirements - by resource type
  - Table of requested/assigned specific resources – by name

A.17 PRODUCT DESCRIPTION

A.17.1 Purpose

A Product Description is used to provide full and accurate details of a product.

A.17.2 Composition

■ **Identifier**   Unique key, probably allocated by the configuration management method and likely to include the project name, item name and version number
■ **Title**   Name by which the product is known
■ **Purpose**   This defines the purpose that the product will fulfil and who will use it
■ **Composition**   This is a list of the parts of the product
■ **Derivation**   What are the source products from which this product is derived?
■ **Format and presentation**   The characteristics of the product

- **Development skills required** An indication of the skills required to develop the product or a pointer to which area(s) should supply the development resources
- **Quality criteria** To what quality specification must the product be produced, and what quality measurements will be applied by those inspecting the finished product?
- **Quality tolerance** Details of any range in the quality criteria within which the product would be acceptable
- **Quality method** The kinds of quality method that are to be used to check the quality or functionality of the product
- **Quality skills required** An indication of the skills required to undertake the quality method or a pointer to which area(s) should supply the checking resources
- **Quality responsibilities** Defining the producer, reviewer(s) and approver(s) for the product.

A.19 PROJECT BRIEF

A.19.1 Purpose

A Project Brief is used to provide a full and firm foundation for the initiation of the project and is created in the Starting up a Project process.

A.19.2 Composition

- **Project definition** Explaining what the project needs to achieve. It should include:
  - Background
  - Project objectives (covering time, cost, quality, scope, risk and benefit performance goals)
  - Desired outcomes
  - Project scope and exclusions

  - Constraints and assumptions
  - Project tolerances
  - The user(s) and any other known interested parties
  - Interfaces
- **Outline Business Case** (see section A.2) Reasons why the project is needed and the business option selected
- **Project Product Description** (see section A.21) Including the customer's quality expectations, user acceptance criteria, and operations and maintenance acceptance criteria
- **Project approach** To define the choice of solution that will be used within the project to deliver the business option selected from the Business Case
- **Project management team structure** A chart showing who will be involved with the project
- **Role descriptions** For the project management team and any other key resources identified at this time
- **References** To any associated documents or products.

A.20 PROJECT INITIATION DOCUMENTATION

A.20.1 Purpose

The purpose of the Project Initiation Documentation is to define the project, in order to form the basis for its management and an assessment of its overall success. The Project Initiation Documentation gives the direction and scope of the project and (along with the Stage Plan) forms the 'contract' between the Project Manager and the Project Board.

A.20.2 Composition

There follows a contents list for the Project Initiation Document. Note that the first two (project definition and project approach) are extracted from the Project Brief.

- **Project definition** Explaining what the project needs to achieve, extracted from the Project Brief
- **Project approach** To define the choice of solution that will be used in the project to deliver the business option selected from the Business Case, extracted from the Project Brief
- **Business Case** (see section A.2) Describing the justification for the project based on estimated costs, risks and benefits
- **Project management team structure** A chart showing who will be involved with the project
- **Role descriptions** For the project management team and any other key resources
- **Quality Management Strategy** Describing the quality techniques and standards to be applied, and the responsibilities for achieving the required quality levels
- **Configuration Management Strategy** Describing how and by whom the project's products will be controlled and protected
- **Risk Management Strategy** Describing the specific risk management techniques and standards to be applied, and the responsibilities for achieving an effective risk management procedure
- **Communication Management Strategy** To define the parties interested in the project and the means and frequency of communication between them and the project
- **Project Plan** (see section A.16) Describing how and when the project's objectives are to be achieved, by showing the major products, activities and resources required on the project
- **Project controls** Summarizing the project-level controls such as stage boundaries, agreed tolerances, monitoring and reporting
- **Tailoring of PRINCE2** A summary of how PRINCE2 will be tailored for the project.

A.21 PROJECT PRODUCT DESCRIPTION

A.21.1 Purpose

The Project Product Description is a special form of Product Description that defines what the project must deliver in order to gain acceptance. It is used to:

- Gain agreement from the user on the project's scope and requirements
- Define the customer's quality expectations
- Define the acceptance criteria, method and responsibilities for the project.

A.21.2 Composition

- **Title** Name by which the project is known
- **Purpose** This defines the purpose that the project's product will fulfil and who will use it
- **Composition** A description of the major products to be delivered by the project
- **Derivation** What are the source products from which this product is derived?
- **Development skills required** An indication of the skills required to develop the product, or a pointer to which area(s) should supply the development resources
- **Customer's quality expectations** A description of the quality expected of the project's product and the standards and processes that will need to be applied to achieve that quality

- **Acceptance criteria**   A prioritized list of criteria that the project's product must meet before the customer will accept it – i.e. measurable definitions of the attributes that must apply to the set of products to be acceptable to key stakeholders (and, in particular, the users and the operational and maintenance organizations)
- **Project-level quality tolerances**   Specifying any tolerances that may apply for the acceptance criteria
- **Acceptance method**   Stating the means by which acceptance will be confirmed
- **Acceptance responsibilities**   Defining who will be responsible for confirming acceptance.

A.26   WORK PACKAGE

A.26.1 Purpose

A Work Package is a set of information about one or more required products collated by the Project Manager to pass responsibility for work or delivery formally to a Team Manager or team member.

A.26.2 Composition

- **Date**   The date of the agreement between the Project Manager and the Team Manager/person authorized
- **Team Manager or person authorized**   The name of the Team Manager or individual with whom the agreement has been made
- **Work Package description**   A description of the work to be done
- **Techniques, processes and procedures**   Any techniques, tools, standards, processes or procedures to be used in the creation of the specialist products

- **Development interfaces**   Interfaces that must be maintained while developing the products
- **Operations and maintenance interfaces**   Identification of any specialist products with which the product(s) in the Work Package will have to interface during their operational life
- **Configuration management requirements**   A statement of any arrangements that must be made by the producer, and who needs to be advised of changes in the status of the Work Package
- **Joint agreements**   Details of the agreements on effort, cost, start and end dates, and key milestones for the Work Package
- **Tolerances**   Details of the tolerances for the Work Package (the tolerances will be for time and cost but may also include scope and risk)
- **Constraints**   Any constraints (apart from the tolerances) on the work, people to be involved, timings, charges, rules to be followed
- **Reporting arrangements**   The expected frequency and content of Checkpoint Reports
- **Problem handling and escalation**   This refers to the procedure for raising issues and risks
- **Extracts or references**   Any extracts or references to related documents, specifically the Stage Plan and Product Description(s)
- **Approval method**   The person, role or group who will approve the completed products within the Work Package, and how the Project Manager is to be advised of completion of the products and Work Package.

Further information

Further information

FROM THE OFFICE OF GOVERNMENT COMMERCE

PRINCE2

PRINCE2 is part of a suite of guidance developed by the Office of Government Commerce (OGC), aimed at helping organizations and individuals manage their projects, programmes and services. Where appropriate, this guidance is supported by a qualification scheme and accredited training and consultancy services.

Managing Successful Projects with PRINCE2 (2009). The Stationery Office, London.

Directing Successful Projects with PRINCE2 (2009). The Stationery Office, London.

Management of Risk (M_o_R®)

Projects exist in a fundamentally uncertain world and, as such, effective management of risk is crucial to managing the delivery of the project's products, their outcomes and the ultimate benefits that have been identified. Management of risk (M_o_R) puts the management of project risk into the context of the wider business environment.

Management of Risk: Guidance for Practitioners (2007). The Stationery Office, London.

Managing Successful Programmes (MSP™)

Managing Successful Programmes represents proven programme management good practice in successfully delivering transformational change across a wide range of public and private sector organizations. It provides a framework to direct and oversee the implementation of a set of related projects and activities in order to deliver outcomes and benefits related to the organization's strategic objectives.

Managing Successful Programmes (2007). The Stationery Office, London.

Portfolio Management Guide

The Portfolio Management Guide explains the key principles of portfolio management, from the experience of public and private sector organizations in the UK and internationally. It provides practical advice on setting up a portfolio management function, illustrated with real-life examples, and concludes with a section on further advice and guidance. The main audience for this guide comprises the teams responsible for coordinating programmes and projects, particularly those providing support for investment decisions and reporting on progress to the management board. A working knowledge of programme and project management and progress reporting is assumed.

Portfolio, Programme and Project Management Maturity Model (P3M3™)

The Portfolio, Programme and Project Management Maturity Model (P3M3) is a reference guide for structured best practice. It breaks down the broad disciplines of portfolio, programme and project management into a hierarchy of perspectives.

The hierarchical approach enables organizations to assess their current capability and then plot a roadmap for improvement prioritized by those perspectives that will make the biggest impact on performance.

Portfolio, Programme and Project Offices (P3O®)

Portfolio, Programme and Project Offices provides guidance on how to define, establish and operate a portfolio, programme or project office. It covers the range of functions and services that P3Os may provide and includes references to the techniques that may be employed.

Portfolio, Programme and Project Offices (2008). The Stationery Office, London.

PRINCE2 Maturity Model (P2MM)

The PRINCE2 Maturity Model (P2MM) describes a set of key process areas (KPAs) required for the effective implementation and use of PRINCE2 within an organization. This is P2MM's core value: while the PRINCE2 manual describes how to manage a single project, it does not include any processes on how to embed PRINCE2, whereas P2MM does.

P2MM describes key practices aligned with the PRINCE2 processes and components to enable repeatable application of the method (Level 2), and goes further to describe the key practices required to institutionalize the method (Level 3) as a standard business process for managing projects.

OGC Gateway Review process

OGC Gateway Review process is a well-established project and programme assurance review process which is mandated for all UK government high-risk programmes and projects. OGC Gateway Review delivers a peer review, in which independent practitioners from outside the individual programme/project use their experience and expertise to examine progress and assess the likelihood of successful delivery of the programme or project. The review process is used to provide a valuable additional perspective on the issues facing the internal team, and an external challenge to the robustness of plans and processes. This service is based on good practice and there are many similar examples across all business sectors of this type of peer review designed to provide assurance to the owner of the programme or project.

Full details of the OGC Gateway Review process are available from the OGC website.

Achieving Excellence in Construction

Achieving Excellence in Construction procurement guidance is contained within a set of 11 guides and two high-level guides. It builds on UK central government departments' recent experience, supports future strategy and aligns with the OGC Gateway Review process.

Through the Achieving Excellence in Construction initiative, central government departments and public sector organizations commit to maximize, by continual improvement, the efficiency, effectiveness and value for money of their procurement of new works, maintenance and refurbishment.

ITIL® Service Management Practices

ITIL is the most widely accepted approach to IT service management in the world. Providing a cohesive set of best-practice guidance drawn from the public and private sectors across the world, it has recently undergone a major and important refresh project.

IT Service Management (ITSM) derives enormous benefits from a best-practice approach. Because ITSM is driven both by technology and the huge range of organizational environments in which it operates, it is in a state of constant evolution. Best practice, based on expert advice and input from ITIL users, is both current and practical, combining the latest thinking with sound, common-sense guidance.

Continual Service Improvement (2007). The Stationery Office, London.

Service Design (2007). The Stationery Office, London.

Service Operation (2007). The Stationery Office, London.

Service Strategy (2007). The Stationery Office, London.

Service Transition (2007). The Stationery Office, London.

FROM THE STATIONERY OFFICE (COMPLEMENTARY PUBLICATIONS)

APMP for PRINCE2 Practitioners

This study guide enables candidates familiar with PRINCE2 to prepare for the APMP exam. It provides APMP exam candidates with a single source of reference material that covers all aspects of the APMP syllabus, including both pre-course and on-course material, whilst aligning it with the PRINCE2 method. This enables PRINCE2 practitioners (or project management staff working within a PRINCE2 environment) to expand their

project management knowledge to cover all topics within the APMP syllabus.

APMP for PRINCE2 Practitioners (2008). The Stationery Office, London.

Focus on Skills series suite (set of three publications)

The Focus on Skills series suite explores the various 'soft skills' that are demonstrated by effective project and programme managers, as the day-to-day coordination, motivation and communication aspects of project and programme management are very similar.

Leadership Skills for Project and Programme Managers (2008). The Stationery Office, London.

Team Management Skills for Project and Programme Managers (2008). The Stationery Office, London.

Communication Skills for Project and Programme Managers (2008). The Stationery Office, London.

Agile Project Management: Running PRINCE2 Projects with DSDM Atern

This ground-breaking publication shows how users can combine the strength of both approaches considered, so that they complement each other and create a new, best-of-breed framework suitable for all project environments. Based on PRINCE2 and DSDM Atern, the two most established and internationally recognized project management approaches, this title explores the differences between the two approaches before showing where they overlap and how they can be integrated. While DSDM Atern is a project management methodology in its own right, this new publication sits within the PRINCE2 suite of titles.

Agile Project Management: Running PRINCE2 Projects with DSDM Atern (2007). The Stationery Office, London.

Improving Project Performance using the PRINCE2 Maturity Model

PRINCE2 is cited as the most widely used project management method worldwide, but, while the PRINCE2 manual describes how to manage a single project, it does not include any guidance on how to embed PRINCE2 into an organization.

Such guidance is now available: this publication describes the organizational processes and practices required for the effective implementation of PRINCE2 as an organizational standard. It includes guidance on assigning ownership, tailoring the method, training, integrating PRINCE2 with other management systems and establishing quality assurance mechanisms to gain a continual improvement capability.

In reading *Improving Project Performance using the PRINCE2 Maturity Model*, you will discover how organizations can gain full value from the PRINCE2 method. It contains practical advice on using the OGC's PRINCE2 Maturity Model (P2MM), and shows how P2MM can be applied in different situations.

Improving Project Performance using the PRINCE2 Maturity Model (2007). The Stationery Office, London.

Accreditation

Having a qualification in PRINCE2 can be a great asset. There are two levels of qualification:

- **Foundation level** This aims to measure whether a candidate could act as an informed member of a project management team on a project using PRINCE2 within an environment supporting PRINCE2. Candidates need to show they understand the principles and terminology of the method.
- **Practitioner level** This aims to measure whether a candidate could apply PRINCE2 to the running and managing of a non-complex project within an environment supporting PRINCE2. Candidates need to show the competence required for the foundation qualification, and show that they can apply and tailor PRINCE2 to address the needs and problems of a given project scenario.

For more information on accredited training organizations for PRINCE2 and the examinations, please visit www.apmgroup.co.uk/PRINCE2

Glossary

Glossary

accept (risk response)

A risk response to a threat where a conscious and deliberate decision is taken to retain the threat, having discerned that it is more economical to do so than to attempt a risk response action. The threat should continue to be monitored to ensure that it remains tolerable.

acceptance

The formal act of acknowledging that the project has met agreed acceptance criteria and thereby met the requirements of its stakeholders.

acceptance criteria

A prioritized list of criteria that the project product must meet before the customer will accept it, i.e. measurable definitions of the attributes required for the set of products to be acceptable to key stakeholders.

activity

A process, function or task that occurs over time, has recognizable results and is managed. It is usually defined as part of a process or plan.

approval

The formal confirmation that a product is complete and meets its requirements (less any concessions) as defined by its Product Description.

approver

The person or group (e.g. a Project Board) who is identified as qualified and authorized to approve a (management or specialist) product as being complete and fit for purpose.

assurance

All the systematic actions necessary to provide confidence that the target (system, process, organization, programme, project, outcome, benefit, capability, product output, deliverable) is appropriate. Appropriateness might be defined subjectively or objectively in different circumstances. The implication is that assurance will have a level of independence from that which is being assured. See also 'Project Assurance' and 'quality assurance'.

authority

The right to allocate resources and make decisions (applies to project, stage and team levels).

authorization

The point at which an authority is granted.

avoid (risk response)

A risk response to a threat where the threat either can no longer have an impact or can no longer happen.

baseline

Reference levels against which an entity is monitored and controlled.

baseline management product

A type of management product that defines aspects of the project and, once approved, is subject to change control.

benefit

The measurable improvement resulting from an outcome perceived as an advantage by one or more stakeholders.

Benefits Review Plan

A plan that defines how and when a measurement of the achievement of the project's benefits can be made. If the project is being managed within a programme, this information may be created and maintained at the programme level.

benefits tolerance

The permissible deviation in the expected benefit that is allowed before the deviation needs to be escalated to the next level of management. Benefits tolerance is documented in the Business Case. See also 'tolerance'.

Business Case

The justification for an organizational activity (project), which typically contains costs, benefits, risks and timescales, and against which continuing viability is tested.

Change Authority

A person or group to which the Project Board may delegate responsibility for the consideration of requests for change or off-specifications. The Change Authority may be given a change budget and can approve changes within that budget.

change budget

The money allocated to the Change Authority available to be spent on authorized requests for change.

change control

The procedure that ensures that all changes that may affect the project's agreed objectives are identified, assessed and either approved, rejected or deferred.

checkpoint

A team-level, time-driven review of progress.

Checkpoint Report

A progress report of the information gathered at a checkpoint, which is given by a team to the Project Manager and which provides reporting data as defined in the Work Package.

closure notification

Advice from the Project Board to inform all stakeholders and the host sites that the project resources can be disbanded and support services, such as space, equipment and access, demobilized. It should indicate a closure date for costs to be charged to the project.

closure recommendation

A recommendation prepared by the Project Manager for the Project Board to send as a project closure notification when the board is satisfied that the project can be closed.

Communication Management Strategy

A description of the means and frequency of communication between the project and the project's stakeholders.

concession

An off-specification that is accepted by the Project Board without corrective action.

configuration item

An entity that is subject to configuration management. The entity may be a component of a product, a product, or a set of products in a release.

Configuration Item Record

A record that describes the status, version and variant of a configuration item, and any details of important relationships between them.

configuration management

Technical and administrative activities concerned with the creation, maintenance and controlled change of configuration throughout the life of a product.

Configuration Management Strategy

A description of how and by whom the project's products will be controlled and protected.

configuration management system

The set of processes, tools and databases that are used to manage configuration data. Typically, a project will use the configuration management system of either the customer or supplier organization.

constraints

The restrictions or limitations that the project is bound by.

corporate or programme standards

These are over-arching standards that the project must adhere to. They will influence the four project strategies (Communication Management Strategy, Configuration Management Strategy, Quality Management Strategy and Risk Management Strategy) and the project controls.

corrective action

A set of actions to resolve a threat to a plan's tolerances or a defect in a product.

cost tolerance

The permissible deviation in a plan's cost that is allowed before the deviation needs to be escalated to the next level of management. Cost tolerance is documented in the respective plan. See also 'tolerance'.

customer

The person or group who commissioned the work and will benefit from the end results.

customer's quality expectations

A statement about the quality expected from the project product, captured in the Project Product Description.

Daily Log

Used to record problems/concerns that can be handled by the Project Manager informally.

deliverable

See 'output'.

dependencies (plan)

The relationship between products or activities. For example, the development of Product C cannot start until Products A and B have been completed. Dependencies can be internal or external.

Internal dependencies are those under the control of the Project Manager. External dependencies are those outside the control of the Project Manager - for example, the delivery of a product required by this project from another project.

dis-benefit

An outcome that is perceived as negative by one or more stakeholders. It is an actual consequence of an activity whereas, by definition, a risk has some uncertainty about whether it will materialize.

embedding (PRINCE2)

What an organization needs to do to adopt PRINCE2 as its corporate project management method. See also, in contrast, 'tailoring', which defines what a project needs to do to apply the method to a specific project environment.

End Project Report

A report given by the Project Manager to the Project Board, that confirms the handover of all products and provides an updated Business Case and an assessment of how well the project has done against the original Project Initiation Documentation.

end stage assessment

The review by the Project Board and Project Manager of the End Stage Report to decide whether to approve the next Stage Plan. According to the size and criticality of the project, the review may be formal or informal. The authority to proceed should be documented as a formal record.

End Stage Report

A report given by the Project Manager to the Project Board at the end of each management stage of the project. This provides information about the project performance during the stage and the project status at stage end.

enhance (risk response)

A risk response to an opportunity where proactive actions are taken to enhance both the probability of the event occurring and the impact of the event should it occur.

event-driven control

A control that takes place when a specific event occurs. This could be, for example, the end of a stage, the completion of the Project Initiation Documentation, or the creation of an Exception Report. It could also include organizational events that may affect the project, such as the end of the financial year.

exception

A situation where it can be forecast that there will be a deviation beyond the tolerance levels agreed between Project Manager and Project Board (or between Project Board and corporate or programme management).

exception assessment

This is a review by the Project Board to approve (or reject) an Exception Plan.

Exception Plan

This is a plan that often follows an Exception Report. For a Stage Plan exception, it covers the period from the present to the end of the current stage. If the exception were at project level, the Project Plan would be replaced.

Exception Report

A description of the exception situation, its impact, options, recommendation and impact of the recommendation. This report is prepared by the Project Manager for the Project Board.

Executive

The single individual with overall responsibility for ensuring that a project meets its objectives and delivers the projected benefits. This individual should ensure that the project maintains its business focus, that it has clear authority, and that the work, including risks, is actively managed. The Executive is the chair of the Project Board. He or she represents the customer and is responsible for the Business Case.

exploit (risk response)

A risk response to an opportunity by seizing the opportunity to ensure that it will happen and that the impact will be realized.

fallback (risk response)

A risk response to a threat by putting in place a fallback plan for the actions that will be taken to reduce the impact of the threat should the risk occur.

follow-on action recommendations

Recommended actions related to unfinished work, ongoing issues and risks, and any other activities needed to take a product to the next phase of its life. These are summarized and included in the End Stage Report (for phased handover) and End Project Report.

handover

The transfer of ownership of a set of products to the respective user(s). The set of products is known as a release. There may be more than one handover in the life of a project (phased delivery). The final handover takes place in the Closing a Project process.

Highlight Report

A time-driven report from the Project Manager to the Project Board on stage progress.

impact (of risk)

The result of a particular threat or opportunity actually occurring, or the anticipation of such a result.

inherent risk

The exposure arising from a specific risk before any action has been taken to manage it.

initiation stage

The period from when the Project Board authorizes initiation to when they authorize the project (or decide not to go ahead with the project). The detailed planning and establishment of the project management infrastructure is covered by the Initiating a Project process.

issue

A relevant event that has happened, was not planned, and requires management action. It can be any concern, query, request for change, suggestion or off-specification raised during a project. Project issues can be about anything to do with the project.

Issue Register

A register used to capture and maintain information on all of the issues that are being managed formally. The Issue Register should be monitored by the Project Manager on a regular basis.

Issue Report

A report containing the description, impact assessment and recommendations for a request for change, off-specification or a problem/concern. It is only created for those issues that need to be handled formally.

Lessons Log

An informal repository for lessons that apply to this project or future projects.

Lessons Report

A report that documents any lessons that can be usefully applied to other projects. The purpose of the report is to provoke action so that the positive lessons from a project become embedded in the organization's way of working and that the organization is able to avoid the negative lessons on future projects.

logs

Informal repositories managed by the Project Manager that do not require any agreement by the Project Board on their format and composition. PRINCE2 has two logs: the Daily Log and the Lessons Log.

management product

A product that will be required as part of managing the project, and establishing and maintaining quality (for example, Highlight Report, End Stage Report etc.). The management products stay constant, whatever the type of project, and can be used as described, or with any relevant modifications, for all projects. There are three types of management product: baselines, records and reports.

management stage

The section of a project that the Project Manager is managing on behalf of the Project Board at any one time, at the end of which the Project Board will wish to review progress to date, the state of the Project Plan, the Business Case and risks, and the next Stage Plan in order to decide whether to continue with the project.

off-specification

Something that should be provided by the project, but currently is not (or is forecast not to be) provided. This might be a missing product or a product not meeting its specifications. It is one type of issue.

operational and maintenance acceptance

A specific type of acceptance by the person or group who will support the product once it is handed over into the operational environment.

outcome

The result of change, normally affecting real-world behaviour and/or circumstances. Outcomes are desired when a change is conceived. They are achieved as a result of the activities undertaken to effect the change.

output

A specialist product that is handed over to a user(s). Note that management products are not outputs but are created solely for the purpose of managing the project.

performance targets

A plan's goals for time, cost, quality, scope, benefits and risk.

plan

A detailed proposal for doing or achieving something which specifies the what, when, how and by whom. In PRINCE2 there are only the following types of plan: Project Plan, Stage Plan, Team Plan, Exception Plan and Benefits Review Plan.

planned closure

The PRINCE2 activity to close a project.

planning horizon

The period of time for which it is possible to accurately plan.

portfolio

All the programmes and stand-alone projects being undertaken by an organization, a group of organizations, or an organizational unit.

premature closure

The PRINCE2 activity to close a project before its planned closure. The Project Manager must ensure that work in progress is not simply abandoned, but that the project salvages any value created to date, and checks that any gaps left by the cancellation of the project are raised to corporate or programme management.

PRINCE2

A method that supports some selected aspects of project management. The acronym stands for PRojects IN Controlled Environments.

PRINCE2 principles

The guiding obligations for good project management practice that form the basis of a project being managed using PRINCE2.

PRINCE2 project

A project that applies the PRINCE2 principles.

probability

This is the evaluated likelihood of a particular threat or opportunity actually happening, including a consideration of the frequency with which this may arise.

problem/concern

A type of issue (other than a request for change or off-specification) that the Project Manager needs to resolve or escalate.

procedure

A series of actions for a particular aspect of project management established specifically for the project – for example, a risk management procedure.

process

A structured set of activities designed to accomplish a specific objective. A process takes one or more defined inputs and turns them into defined outputs.

producer

The person or group responsible for developing a product.

product

An input or output, whether tangible or intangible, that can be described in advance, created and tested. PRINCE2 has two types of products – management products and specialist products.

product breakdown structure

A hierarchy of all the products to be produced during a plan.

product checklist

A list of the major products of a plan, plus key dates in their delivery.

Product Description

A description of a product's purpose, composition, derivation and quality criteria. It is produced at planning time, as soon as possible after the need for the product is identified.

product flow diagram

A diagram showing the sequence of production and interdependencies of the products listed in a product breakdown structure.

Product Status Account

A report on the status of products. The required products can be specified by identifier or the part of the project in which they were developed.

product-based planning

A technique leading to a comprehensive plan based on the creation and delivery of required outputs. The technique considers prerequisite products, quality requirements and the dependencies between products.

programme

A temporary flexible organization structure created to coordinate, direct and oversee the implementation of a set of related projects and activities in order to deliver outcomes and benefits related to the organization's strategic objectives. A programme is likely to have a life that spans several years.

project

A temporary organization that is created for the purpose of delivering one or more business products according to an agreed Business Case.

project approach

A description of the way in which the work of the project is to be approached. For example, are we building a product from scratch or buying in a product that already exists?

Project Assurance

The Project Board's responsibilities to assure itself that the project is being conducted correctly. The Project Board members each have a specific area of focus for Project Assurance, namely business assurance for the Executive, user assurance for the Senior User(s), and supplier assurance for the Senior Supplier(s).

project authorization notification

Advice from the Project Board to inform all stakeholders and the host sites that the project has been authorized and to request any necessary logistical support (e.g. communication facilities, equipment and any Project Support) sufficient for the duration of the project.

Project Brief

Statement that describes the purpose, cost, time and performance requirements, and constraints for a project. It is created pre-project during the Starting up a Project process and is used during the Initiating a Project process to create the Project Initiation Documentation and its components. It is superseded by the Project Initiation Documentation and not maintained.

Project Initiation Documentation

A logical set of documents that brings together the key information needed to start the project on a sound basis and that conveys the information to all concerned with the project.

project initiation notification

Advice from the Project Board to inform all stakeholders and the host sites that the project is being initiated and to request any necessary logistical support (e.g. communication facilities, equipment and any Project Support) sufficient for the initiation stage.

project lifecycle

The period from the start-up of a project to the acceptance of the project product.

project management

The planning, delegating, monitoring and control of all aspects of the project, and the motivation of those involved, to achieve the project objectives within the expected performance targets for time, cost, quality, scope, benefits and risks.

project management team

The entire management structure of the Project Board, and Project Manager, plus any Team Manager, Project Assurance and Project Support roles.

project management team structure

An organization chart showing the people assigned to the project management team roles to be used, and their delegation and reporting relationships.

Project Manager

The person given the authority and responsibility to manage the project on a day-to-day basis to deliver the required products within the constraints agreed with the Project Board.

project mandate

An external product generated by the authority commissioning the project that forms the trigger for Starting up a Project.

project office

A temporary office set up to support the delivery of a specific change initiative being delivered as a project. If used, the project office undertakes the responsibility of the Project Support role.

residual risk

The risk remaining after the risk response has been applied.

reviewer

A person or group independent of the producer who assesses whether a product meets its requirements as defined in its Product Description.

risk

An uncertain event or set of events that, should it occur, will have an effect on the achievement of objectives. A risk is measured by a combination of the probability of a perceived threat or opportunity occurring, and the magnitude of its impact on objectives.

risk actionee

A nominated owner of an action to address a risk. Some actions may not be within the remit of the risk owner to control explicitly; in that situation there should be a nominated owner of the action to address the risk. He or she will need to keep the risk owner apprised of the situation.

risk appetite

An organization's unique attitude towards risk taking that in turn dictates the amount of risk that it considers is acceptable.

risk estimation

The estimation of probability and impact of an individual risk, taking into account predetermined standards, target risk levels, interdependencies and other relevant factors.

risk evaluation

The process of understanding the net effect of the identified threats and opportunities on an activity when aggregated together.

risk management

The systematic application of principles, approaches and processes to the tasks of identifying and assessing risks, and then planning and implementing risk responses.

Risk Management Strategy

A strategy describing the goals of applying risk management, as well as the procedure that will be adopted, roles and responsibilities, risk tolerances, the timing of risk management interventions, the tools and techniques that will be used, and the reporting requirements.

risk owner

A named individual who is responsible for the management, monitoring and control of all aspects of a particular risk assigned to them, including the implementation of the selected responses to address the threats or to maximize the opportunities.

risk profile

A description of the types of risk that are faced by an organization and its exposure to those risks.

Risk Register

A record of identified risks relating to an initiative, including their status and history.

risk response

Actions that may be taken to bring a situation to a level where exposure to risk is acceptable to the organization. These responses fall into a number of risk response categories.

risk response category

A category of risk response. For threats, the individual risk response category can be avoid, reduce, transfer, accept or share. For opportunities, the individual risk response category can be exploit, enhance, reject or share.

risk tolerance

The threshold levels of risk exposure which, when exceeded, will trigger an Exception Report to bring the situation to the attention of the Project Board. Risk tolerances could include limits on the plan's aggregated risks (e.g. cost of aggregated threats to remain less than 10% of the plan's budget), or limits on any individual threat (e.g. any threat to operational service). Risk tolerance is documented in the Risk Management Strategy.

role description

A description of the set of responsibilities specific to a role.

schedule

Graphical representation of a plan (for example, a Gantt chart), typically describing a sequence of tasks, together with resource allocations, which collectively deliver the plan. In PRINCE2, project activities should only be documented in the schedules associated with a Project Plan, Stage Plan or Team Plan. Actions that are allocated from day-to-day management may be documented in the relevant project log (i.e. Risk Register, Daily Log, Issue Register, Quality Register) if they do not require significant activity.

scope

For a plan, the sum total of its products and the extent of their requirements. It is described by the product breakdown structure for the plan and associated Product Descriptions.

scope tolerance

The permissible deviation in a plan's scope that is allowed before the deviation needs to be escalated to the next level of management. Scope tolerance is documented in the respective plan in the form of a note or reference to the product breakdown structure for that plan. See 'tolerance'.

Senior Responsible Owner

A UK government term for the individual responsible for ensuring that a project or programme of change meets its objectives and delivers the projected benefits. The person should be the owner of the overall business change that is being supported by the project. The Senior Responsible Owner (SRO) should ensure that the change maintains its business focus, that it has clear authority, and that the context, including risks, is actively managed. This individual must be senior and must take personal responsibility for successful delivery of the project. The SRO should be recognized as the owner throughout the organization.

The SRO appoints the project's Executive (or in some cases may elect to be the Executive).

Senior Supplier

The Project Board role that provides knowledge and experience of the main discipline(s) involved in the production of the project's deliverable(s). The Senior Supplier represents the supplier interests within the project and provides supplier resources.

Senior User

The Project Board role accountable for ensuring that user needs are specified correctly and that the solution meets those needs.

specialist product

A product whose development is the subject of the plan. The specialist products are specific to an individual project (for example, an advertising campaign, a car park ticketing system, foundations for a building, a new business process etc.) Also known as a deliverable or output.

sponsor

The main driving force behind a programme or project. PRINCE2 does not define a role for the sponsor, but the sponsor is most likely to be the Executive on the Project Board, or the person who has appointed the Executive.

stage

See 'management stage' or 'technical stage'.

Stage Plan

A detailed plan used as the basis for project management control throughout a stage.

stakeholder

Any individual, group or organization that can affect, be affected by, or perceive itself to be affected by, an initiative (programme, project, activity, risk).

start-up

The pre-project activities undertaken by the Executive and the Project Manager to produce the outline Business Case, Project Brief and Initiation Stage Plan.

strategy

An approach or line to take, designed to achieve a long-term aim. Strategies can exist at different levels – at the corporate, programme and project level. At the project level, PRINCE2 defines four strategies: Communication Management Strategy, Configuration Management Strategy, Quality Management Strategy and Risk Management Strategy.

supplier

The person, group or groups responsible for the supply of the project's specialist products.

tailoring

The appropriate use of PRINCE2 on any given project, ensuring that there is the correct amount of planning, control, governance and use of the processes and themes (whereas the adoption of PRINCE2 across an organization is known as 'embedding').

Team Manager

The person responsible for the production of those products allocated by the Project Manager (as defined in a Work Package) to an appropriate quality, timescale and at a cost acceptable to the Project Board. This role reports to, and takes direction from, the Project Manager. If a Team Manager is not assigned, then the Project Manager undertakes the responsibilities of the Team Manager role.

Team Plan

An optional level of plan used as the basis for team management control when executing Work Packages.

technical stage

A method of grouping work together by the set of techniques used, or the products created. This results in stages covering elements such as design, build and implementation. Such stages are technical stages and are a separate concept from management stages.

theme

An aspect of project management that needs to be continually addressed, and that requires specific treatment for the PRINCE2 processes to be effective.

time tolerance

The permissible deviation in a plan's time that is allowed before the deviation needs to be escalated to the next level of management. Time tolerance is documented in the respective plan. See also 'tolerance'.

time-driven control

A management control that is periodic in nature, to enable the next higher authority to monitor progress – e.g. a control that takes place every two weeks. PRINCE2 offers two key time-driven progress reports: Checkpoint Report and Highlight Report.

tolerance

The permissible deviation above and below a plan's target for time and cost without escalating the deviation to the next level of management. There may also be tolerance levels for quality, scope, benefit and risk. Tolerance is applied at project, stage and team levels.

transfer (risk response)

A response to a threat where a third party takes on responsibility for some of the financial impact of the threat (for example, through insurance or by means of appropriate clauses in a contract).

trigger

An event or decision that triggers a PRINCE2 process.

user

The person or group who will use one or more of the project's products.

user acceptance

A specific type of acceptance by the person or group who will use the product once it is handed over into the operational environment.

version

A specific baseline of a product. Versions typically use naming conventions that enable the sequence or date of the baseline to be identified. For example, Project Plan version 2 is the baseline after Project Plan version 1.

Work Package

The set of information relevant to the creation of one or more products. It will contain a description of the work, the Product Description(s), details of any constraints on production, and confirmation of the agreement between the Project Manager and the person or Team Manager who is to implement the Work Package that the work can be done within the constraints.

Index

Index

Figures are indicated by **bold** page numbers, tables by *italic* numbers.